FDA Regulation of Tobacco Products

FDA Regulation of Tobacco Products

Victoria C. Lockwood
Editor

Nova Science Publishers, Inc.
New York

LIBRARY OF CONGRESS CATALOGING-IN-PUBLICATION DATA
Available upon request.

ISBN 978-1-60692-550-8

Published by Nova Science Publishers, Inc. ✢ New York

CONTENTS

Preface		**vii**
Chapter 1	FDA Regulation of Tobacco Products: A Historical, Policy, and Legal Analysis *C. Stephen Redhead and Vanessa K. Burrows*	**1**
Chapter 2	Tobacco: Selected Legal Issues *Vanessa Burrows*	**67**
Chapter 3	Statement of Andrew C. von Eschenbach, Commissioner of Food and Drugs Before Subcommittee on Health, Committee on Energy and Commerce, United States House of Representatives on 'H.R. 1108, Family Smoking Prevention and Tobacco Control Act'(October 3, 2007)	**87**
Index		**95**

PREFACE

Last year, lawmakers reintroduced bipartisan, bicameral legislation (H.R. 1108, S. 625) to give the Food and Drug Administration (FDA) broad new authority to regulate the manufacture, distribution, advertising, promotion, sale, and use of cigarettes and smokeless tobacco products. Amended versions of both bills have been reported out of committee and await floor action in their respective chambers. The Secretary of Health and Human Services has stated in a July 21, 2008, letter that the Bush Administration "would strongly oppose this legislation." The Family Smoking Prevention and Tobacco Control Act was first introduced in the 108th Congress, the product of lengthy negotiations in which lawmakers sought to balance the competing interests of public health groups and Philip Morris, the nation's leading cigarette company. While these organizations support the legislation, the FDA Commissioner, other tobacco manufacturers, and tobacco industry and convenience store associations have expressed concerns about the bills, which would create a new Chapter IX in the Federal Food, Drug, and Cosmetic Act (FFDCA) solely for the regulation of tobacco products. Among their many provisions, the measures would authorize FDA to: restrict tobacco advertising and promotions, especially to children; develop standards that require changes in tobacco product composition and design, such as the reduction or elimination of toxic chemicals; and require manufacturers to obtain agency approval in order to make reduced-risk and reduced-exposure claims for their products. In the mid-1990s, FDA claimed authority under the FFDCA to regulate cigarettes and smokeless tobacco products as delivery devices for nicotine, an addictive drug. The agency's 1996 tobacco regulation was invalidated by the U.S. Supreme Court in March 2000. The Court concluded that Congress had clearly intended to preclude FDA from regulating tobacco products. It found that because the FFDCA prohibits the marketing of products that have not been found to be safe and effective, the statute would have required FDA to ban such manifestly harmful products as cigarettes and smokeless tobacco if the agency had jurisdiction over them. Such a ban, argued the Court, would plainly contradict congressional intent. The Supreme Court's decision made it clear the Congress would have to enact legislation giving FDA statutory authority over tobacco products in order for the agency to assert jurisdiction. Lawmakers first drafted such language in the 105th Congress as part of legislation to implement the 1997 proposed national tobacco settlement.

In: FDA Regulation of Tobacco Products ISBN: 978-1-60692-550-8
Editor: Victoria C. Lockwood, pp. 1-49

Chapter 1

FDA Regulation of Tobacco Products: A Historical, Policy, and Legal Analysis*

C. Stephen Redhead
Health Policy, Domestic Social Policy Division
Vanessa K. Burrows
American Law Division

Summary

Last year, lawmakers reintroduced bipartisan, bicameral legislation (H.R. 1108, S. 625) to give the Food and Drug Administration (FDA) broad new authority to regulate the manufacture, distribution, advertising, promotion, sale, and use of cigarettes and smokeless tobacco products. Amended versions of both bills have been reported out of committee and await floor action in their respective chambers. The Secretary of Health and Human Services has stated in a July 21,2008, letter that the Bush Administration "would strongly oppose this legislation." The Family Smoking Prevention and Tobacco Control Act was first introduced in the 108th Congress, the product of lengthy negotiations in which lawmakers sought to balance the competing interests of public health groups and Philip Morris, the nation's leading cigarette company. While these organizations support the legislation, the FDA Commissioner, other tobacco manufacturers, and tobacco industry and convenience store associations have expressed concerns about the bills, which would create a new Chapter IX in the Federal Food, Drug,

* Excerpted from CRS Report RL32619, Updated July 30, 2008

and Cosmetic Act (FFDCA) solely for the regulation of tobacco products. Among their many provisions, the measures would authorize FDA to: restrict tobacco advertising and promotions, especially to children; develop standards that require changes in tobacco product composition and design, such as the reduction or elimination of toxic chemicals; and require manufacturers to obtain agency approval in order to make reduced-risk and reduced-exposure claims for their products.

In the mid-1990s, FDA claimed authority under the FFDCA to regulate cigarettes and smokeless tobacco products as delivery devices for nicotine, an addictive drug. The agency's 1996 tobacco regulation was invalidated by the U.S. Supreme Court in March 2000. The Court concluded that Congress had clearly intended to preclude FDA from regulating tobacco products. It found that because the FFDCA prohibits the marketing of products that have not been found to be safe and effective, the statute would have required FDA to ban such manifestly harmful products as cigarettes and smokeless tobacco if the agency had jurisdiction over them. Such a ban, argued the Court, would plainly contradict congressional intent. The Supreme Court's decision made it clear the Congress would have to enact legislation giving FDA statutory authority over tobacco products in order for the agency to assert jurisdiction. Lawmakers first drafted such language in the 105th Congress as part of legislation to implement the 1997 proposed national tobacco settlement.

Under H.R. 1108/S. 625, FDA would be authorized to regulate tobacco product marketing and impose mandatory design changes on tobacco products if it determined that such actions were appropriate for the protection of public health, based on a consideration of the risks and benefits to individual consumers and to the population as a whole. But the legislation would also place certain restrictions on that authority, permitting most existing products to remain on the market (at least in the near term) and reserving for Congress the power to ban tobacco products. For additional information on legal issues involving tobacco, see CRS Report RL33719, Tobacco: Selected Legal Issues, by Vanessa K. Burrows.

Introduction

On February 15,2007, Representatives Henry Waxman (D-C A) and Tom Davis (R-VA) and Senators Ted Kennedy (D-MA) and John Cornyn (R-TX) introduced the Family Smoking Prevention and Tobacco Control Act (H.R. 1108, S. 625). The Senate Health, Education, Labor, and Pensions (HELP) Committee approved S. 625 by a vote of 13-8 on August 1, 2007. On April 2, 2008, the House Energy and Commerce Committee passed H.R. 1108 by a vote of 38-12. While the two measures are broadly similar, H.R. 1108, as reported by the committee, includes several additional provisions intended to address the concerns of various stakeholder groups. Both bills are awaiting floor action in their respective chambers. The legislation would create a new Chapter LX in the

Federal Food, Drug, and Cosmetic Act (FFDCA)[1] giving the FDA broad new authority to regulate the manufacture, distribution, advertising, promotion, sale, and use of cigarettes and smokeless tobacco (i.e., snuff and chewing tobacco). Specifically, the legislation would:

- require all tobacco product manufacturers to register annually with the FDA and provide the agency with a detailed product list;
- mandate biennial inspection of all registered establishments;
- require premarket approval of new tobacco products unless they were determined to be substantially equivalent to other tobacco products already on the market;
- require manufacturers to obtain FDA approval in order to make reduced-risk and reduced-exposure claims for their products, including the use of descriptors such as "light," "mild," and "low";
- authorize FDA to regulate the advertising and promotion of tobacco products in order to protect public health;
- give FDA the authority to modify the composition of tobacco products in order to protect public health (though it would prohibit FDA from eliminating nicotine or banning tobacco products);
- require FDA to develop new regulations for the testing, reporting, and public disclosure of tobacco product ingredients and smoke constituents;
- preserve the authority of states and localities to take additional measures to restrict the distribution, advertising, promotion, sale, access to, and use of tobacco products;
- instruct FDA to issue new recordkeeping requirements to help counter the illicit trade of tobacco products; and
- assess user fees on manufacturers to pay for the cost of FDA tobacco regulation.

In addition, H.R. 1108/S. 625 would require FDA to reissue most of its 1996 tobacco regulation as a final rule, including a ban on outdoor advertising within 1,000 feet of a school or public playground, which is similar to a provision in a Massachusetts regulation that the U.S. Supreme Court previously held unconstitutional.[2] In its 1996 final rule, the agency had claimed jurisdiction over tobacco products under the FFDCA, based on its conclusion that cigarettes and smokeless tobacco products are delivery devices for nicotine, an addictive drug.

---

[1] 21 U.S.C. §§ 301 et seq.
[2] Lorillard Tobacco Co. v. Reilly, 533 U.S. 525 (2001). See infra pages 23-28.

However, in 2000, the U. S. Supreme Court invalidated the FDA tobacco regulation. In a 5-4 decision, the Court ruled in FDA v. Brown & Williamson that FDA does not have the authority under the FFDCA to regulate cigarettes and smokeless tobacco products as drug-delivery devices.[3] The Court based its ruling on the finding that Congress has precluded the FDA from asserting jurisdiction over tobacco products. According to the Court, such authority would be inconsistent with the congressional intent clearly expressed in the FFDCA's overall regulatory scheme and in other tobacco-related legislation. For example, the Court concluded that if the FDA asserted jurisdiction under the FFDCA, it would have no choice but to prohibit the marketing of such harmful products. A ban on tobacco products, argued the Court, would plainly contradict congressional policy, which permits tobacco companies to market their products with limited oversight by the Federal Trade Commission (FTC). In addition, the Court noted that Congress had, in enacting other tobacco-specific legislation, repeatedly rejected proposals to grant the FDA authority over tobacco, thereby demonstrating the intent to deny the agency such jurisdiction.

The Supreme Court's decision ended a four-year legal challenge by the tobacco industry to overturn the FDA regulation. The ruling made it clear that Congress would have to enact legislation giving FDA explicit statutory authority over tobacco products in order for the agency to assert jurisdiction. Lawmakers first drafted such language in the 105th Congress and included it in legislation that would have implemented thel997 proposed national tobacco settlement. That legislation was debated and rejected by the Senate in 1998. Following the Supreme Court's ruling, several lawmakers introduced FDA tobacco legislation in the 107th Congress without subsequent legislative action.[4]

The Family Smoking Prevention and Tobacco Control Act was first introduced by Representatives Davis and Waxman and Senators DeWine (R-OH) and Kennedy in the 108th Congress (H.R. 4433, S. 2461). Its introduction followed months of negotiations in which lawmakers sought to balance the competing interests of public health groups and the tobacco industry. Public health groups and some in the tobacco industry support giving FDA the authority to regulate cigarettes and smokelesstobacco products, but they disagree on the central question of how much regulatory control the agency should be given.

Public health advocates want FDA to have broad authority to take whatever actions the agency considers necessary to protect public health. They argue that giving FDA limited authority would invite tobacco companies to mount a legal

[3] FDA v. Brown & Williamson Tobacco Corp., 529 U.S. 120 (2000).

[4] H.R. 1044 (Waxman); H.R. 1097 (Ganske); H.R. 2180 (Davis); S. 190 (Frist); S. 247 (Harkin); and S. 2626 (Kennedy).

challenge to every proposed regulatory action and would shield tobacco companies from liability. A weak FDA tobacco bill would, in their view, be worse than no bill at all. The tobacco companies, on the other hand, want to see certain restrictions placed on FDA's authority. They oppose giving FDA the authority to alter the composition of their products to the point that adult smokers reject them. The companies want to reserve for Congress — not the FDA — the authority to remove nicotine from tobacco products or take any other action that might lead to the elimination of tobacco products.

The Family Smoking Prevention and Tobacco Control Act represents a compromise between those two competing positions. Leading public health groups and Philip Morris, the nation's largest cigarette manufacturer with 51% of the U.S. market, strongly support the bill's regulatory framework.[5] The other major cigarette companies however, have broken ranks with Philip Morris and are opposed to the legislation.[6] While they continue in principle to support FDA regulation of their products, they fear that the sweeping new regulatory authority outlined in the legislation, including tight restrictions on marketing, will help further consolidate Philip Morris's dominance over the U.S. market.[7]

This report examines the legislative debate over giving FDA the authority to regulate tobacco products and provides some analysis of H.R. 1108/S. 625. It begins with an overview of the FDA's 1996 tobacco rule that includes a summary of the agency's arguments for assertingjurisdiction over tobacco products. That is followed by an analysis of the U.S. Supreme Court decision in FDA v. Brown & Williamson, which overturned the FDA tobacco rule. The report then reviews the 1997 proposed national tobacco settlement, which would have codified the FDA rule and given the agency explicit authority to regulate tobacco products as medical devices. It includes a discussion of the FDA provisions in the McCain tobacco bill (see Table 1), which was introduced and debated in the 105th Congress in an attempt to implement the proposed settlement. The final section of the report summarizes the legislative history and provisions of H.R. 1108/S. 625 (see Table 2), and discusses some of the key issues, including preemption and the regulation of reduced-risk products.

---

[5] Andrew Martin, Trying Again for a Bill to Limit Tobacco Ads, N.Y. Times, February 16, 2007, at C2.

[6] Joe Crea, Big Tobacco Companies Battle over Altria-Backed Bill to Impose FDA Regulation, Legal Times, May 1, 2007.

[7] Lorillard Tobacco Company, FAQs, Does Lorillard favor government regulation of its products? [http://www.lorillard.com/index.php?id=6#70]; R.J. Reynolds Tobacco Company, Should the FDA Regulate Cigarettes? [http://www.rjrt.com/legal/fedFDA.asp].

FDA's 1996 Tobacco Regulation

On August 28, 1996, the FDA issued a final rule aimed at reducing underage smoking and use of smokeless tobacco products.[8] The FDA rule included three sets of provisions: restrictions on the sale and distribution of tobacco products to minors; limits on tobacco-product marketing and advertising; and new labeling requirements for packaging and advertising (see box on next page). The agency said that the purpose of the rule was to reduce the easy access to tobacco products by minors. It also hoped to reduce the amount of positive advertising imagery used by manufacturers to make their products appealing to minors. While the rule did not directly address adult tobacco use, data from the National Survey on Drug Use and Health (NSDUH) suggest that over time it would help reduce adult tobacco consumption. NSDUH data indicate that most smokers take up the habit as teenagers. Thus, reducing the number of new teenage smokers, who are needed to replace adult smokers that quit or die, is expected to lower overall tobacco consumption in the future.

In a written statement issued on October 3, 2007, FDA Commissioner Andrew von Eschenbach expressed concerns with the requirement in H.R. 1108/S. 625 that the agency reissue the 1996 rule.[9] He noted that the rule would rely "on data and information that are a decade old and would need to be updated to reflect the latest science."[10] Additionally, Commissioner von Eschenbach asserted that the bills' timeframes for issuing regulations were "unworkable."[11] Congress sometimes includes short deadlines in order to hasten agency rulemaking.[12]

---

[8] 61 Fed. Reg. 44396-45318; 21 C.F.R. Parts 801, 803, 804, 807, 820, and 897.

[9] H.R. 1108, Family Smoking Prevention and Tobacco Control Act, Hearing Before the Subcomm. on Health of the H. Comm. on Energy and Commerce, 110th Cong. (October 3. 2007) (written statement of Andrew C. von Eschenbach, Commissioner of Food and Drugs. FDA), [http://www.fda.gov/ola/2007/tobaccol00307.html].

[10] Id. The dissenting views to the House Committee on Energy and Commerce also express concerns regarding the codification of the 1996 rule. H.Rept. 110-762, at 159 (2008).

[11] H.R. 1108, Family Smoking Prevention and Tobacco Control Act, Hearing Before the Subcomm. on Health of the H. Comm. on Energy and Commerce, 110th Cong. (October 3, 2007) (written statement of Andrew C. von Eschenbach, Commissioner of Food and Drugs, FDA), [http://www.fda.gov/ola/2007/tobacco100307.html].

[12] See Jeffrey S. Lubbers, A Guide to Federal Agency Rulemaking, 15 (4th ed. 2006).

Summary of FDA's Tobacco Rule

Youth Access Restrictions

- Prohibited the sale of cigarettes or smokeless tobacco to persons under age 18.
- Required retailers to check photo ID to verify age of purchasers under age 27.
- Required that retail sales be conducted in a direct, face-to-face exchange.
- Prohibited the sale or distribution of individual cigarettes.
- Required the sale and distribution of cigarettes in packs of at least 20.
- Prohibited tobacco-product vending machines except in adult-only facilities.
- Prohibited self-service displays of tobacco products except in adult-only facilities.
- Prohibited free samples of cigarettes and smokeless tobacco.

Labeling Requirements

- Required cigarette and smokeless tobacco packaging to include the statement: "Nicotine-Delivery Device for Persons 18 and Older."
- Required cigarette and smokeless tobacco advertising to include the statement: "Nicotine-Delivery Device for Persons 18 and Older."

Advertising and Promotion Restrictions

- Prohibited outdoor advertising (e.g., billboards, posters, placards) within 1,000 feet of a school or playground.
- Limited advertising in publications with significant youth readership to a black-on-white, text-only format.[a]
- Limited advertising in audio format to words with no music or sound effects.
- Limited advertising in video format to static, black-on-white text.
- Prohibited the use of a non-tobacco trade or brand name as a tobacco product brand name, unless that tobacco product brand name existed on January 1, 1995.
- Prohibited the marketing, licensing, distribution, or sale of all non-tobacco items and services identified with a cigarette or smokeless tobacco brand name (e.g., promotional tee shirts and caps).

- Prohibited gifts, credits, and coupons linked to the purchase of tobacco products.
- Prohibited brand-name sponsorship of sporting and other cultural events.

a. The FDA rule defined significant youth readership as having 2 million or more readers under age 18, or having readers under age 18 constitute more than 15% of the total readership.

FDA's Assertion of Jurisdiction over Tobacco Products

Under the FFDC A, drug and device manufacturers must demonstrate that their products are both safe and effective in order to gain FDA marketing approval. The safety and effectiveness standard poses a difficult challenge for regulating tobacco products, which are manifestly unsafe when used as intended. Critics of FDA's rule argued that in asserting regulatory authority over tobacco products, the agency would have no choice but to ban them because of their harmful and addictive effects. In its rulemaking, the FDA conceded that tobacco products are "unsafe" as that term is generally understood, but concluded that banning tobacco products was not a realistic option because the health care system would be overwhelmed by more than 40 million nicotine addicts seeking assistance for withdrawal symptoms. Moreover, the agency argued, banning cigarettes would create an enormous black market, which might lead to the use of unregulated and potentially even more dangerous products.

The FDA asserted jurisdiction over cigarettes and smokeless tobacco by concluding that nicotine is a drug and that cigarettes and smokeless tobacco are drug-delivery devices under the FFDCA's definitions. The statute defines a drug, in relevant part, as "... articles (other than food) intended to affect the structure or any function of the body."[13] In its rulemaking, the FDA drew on the extensive scientific literature documenting nicotine's pharmacologic effects on the body, including satisfaction of addiction, stimulation, and sedation. The agency also concluded that cigarettes and smokeless tobacco are devices that deliver nicotine into the body. As with drugs, the FFDCA's definition of medical devices includes articles that are intended by the manufacturer to affect the structure and function of the body.[14] Unlike a drug, however, a device is defined, in part, as an article "which does not achieve its primary intended purpose through chemical action."[15]

[13] 21 U.S.C. § 321(g)(1)(C); FFDCA § 201(g)(1)(C) (emphasis added).
[14] 21 U.S.C. § 321(h)(3); FFDCA § 201(h)(3).
[15] 21 U.S.C. § 321(h); FFDCA § 201(h).

In the absence of direct claims by the manufacturers about the intended use of tobacco products, the FDA relied on other lines of evidence in order to meet this key definitional criterion for drugs and devices. For example, the agency considered evidence of foreseeability (i.e., a reasonable manufacturer would foresee that consumers will use the product to satisfy nicotine addiction) and actual consumer use (i.e., consumers use the product because they are addicted). FDA officials combed through thousands of pages of internal tobacco company documents before concluding that the manufacturers intended their products to be addictive.

Having made the determination that tobacco products fall under the statutory definitions of drugs and devices, the FDA further concluded that these products are combination products since they have components that are both a drug and a device. Under the FFDCA, the FDA is authorized to regulate products that "constitute a combination of a drug, device, or biologic product."[16] The agency has interpreted this provision as giving it the discretion to regulate combination products as drugs, as devices, or as biologic products.[17] In its final rule, the FDA chose to regulate tobacco products under the device provisions of the FFDCA because they offer the agency greater regulatory flexibility than do the drug provisions of the act.[18]

The device authorities of the act present a range of regulatory controls that apply to all devices. The FDA stated in its rule that these mandatory controls would apply to cigarettes and smokeless tobacco products. They include, among others, adulteration and misbranding provisions, labeling requirements, establishment registration, device listing and premarket notification, recordkeeping and reporting requirements, and good manufacturing practices. The act also requires the agency to classify each device based upon the degree of risk it poses to the user as well as other regulatory concerns and unique qualities of the device. The FDA indicated in the final rule that it would classify cigarettes and smokeless tobacco as either Class I, II, or III devices at some point in the future. The agency further stated that when classification was determined, it would impose any additional requirements that were appropriate.[19]

---

[16] 21 U.S.C. § 353(g); FFDCA § 503(g).
[17] 61 Fed. Reg. 44396, 44400 (1996).
[18] Id. at 44403.
[19] Class I devices (e.g., elastic bandages, manual surgical instruments) present minimal harm to the user and are only subject to general controls, such as manufacturer registration, and labeling. Class II devices (e.g., cardiac pressure monitors, powered surgical instruments) are those forwhich general controls alone are insufficient to assure safety and effectiveness. In addition to complying with general controls, Class II devices are also subject to special controls, such as additional labeling requirements, mandatory performance standards, and postmarket

In addition to mandatory controls, the FFDCA contains various discretionary provisions that apply to devices under certain circumstances. The FDA predicated its authority to regulate tobacco products on one such provision regarding restricted devices. The act's restricted device provision states, in relevant part, that "[t]he Secretary may by regulation require that a device be restricted to sale, distribution, or use ... upon such other conditions as the Secretary may prescribe in such regulation, if, because of its potentialityfor harmful effect or the collateral measures necessary for its use, the Secretary determines that there cannot otherwise be reasonable assurance of its safety and effectiveness."[20]

In the final tobacco rule, the FDA relied on the FFDCA's restricted device provision when it concluded that, because of the harmful effects of cigarettes and smokeless tobacco and in the absence of a reasonable assurance of the safety and effectiveness of such products, it needed to implement additional restrictions on tobacco access and advertising in order to prevent new users from becoming addicted.[21] As a result, the FDA used its restricted device authority to limit youth access to tobacco products. Agency officials also concluded that the authority under the FFDCA's restricted device provision was broad enough to permit the FDA to restrict tobacco-product marketing and advertising. It reasoned that without advertising restrictions, the access restrictions would be substantially diminished if manufacturers were "free to entice children and adolescents to circumvent the access restrictions."[22]

Court Challenge of the FDA Tobacco Rule

The tobacco companies filed a lawsuit against the FDA and sought summary judgment on the grounds that the FDA lacked the authority to regulate tobacco products when such products are marketed and sold without explicit claims of therapeutic benefit. The lawsuit further charged that the FDA exceeded its statutory authority because the FFDCA does not authorize the FDA to regulate tobacco products as drugs or devices.[23] Finally, the companies argued that the

surveillance. Class III devices (e.g., replacement heart valves, breast implants) present the greatest potential for risk of illness or injury and are subject to the most stringent regulatory control. They require premarket approval by FDA — a process that involves a comprehensive agency review of their safety and effectiveness — unless they are substantially equivalent to a device already on the market.

[20] 21 U.S.C. § 360j(e); FFDCA § 520(e) (emphasis added).

[21] 61 Fed. Reg. 44396, 44405.

[22] 61 Fed. Reg. 44406-07.

[23] Coyne Beahm, Inc. v. FDA, 966 F. Supp. 1374 (M.D.N.C. 1997).

rule's advertising restrictions, which limited advertisements to which children are exposed to a black-on-white, text-only format, violated the First Amendment protection of commercial speech.

U.S. District Court (Coyne Beahm, Inc. v. FDA)

On April 25, 1997, a North Carolina federal district court ruled in favor of the FDA, holding that the agency had acted appropriately under the FFDCA when it classified nicotine as a drug and tobacco products as drug-delivery devices.[24] However, while the court upheld the rule's access restrictions and labeling requirements, it ruled that the FDA did not have the authority to restrict tobacco advertising and promotion. The court permitted the two youth access provisions that had taken effect prior to its ruling to remain in effect, but delayed implementation of the rule's other provisions, pending further action by the court.[25] Both sides appealed the district court's ruling.

Federal Court of Appeals (Brown & Williamson Tobacco Corp. v. FDA)

On August 14, 1998, a three-judge panel of the U.S. Court of Appeals for the Fourth Circuit overturned the lower court's decision and ruled that the FDA lacked the statutory authority to regulate tobacco products.[26] The court held that the decision to regulate cigarettes as a restricted device rather than as a drug, in order to avoid having to ban them, was "... obvious sophistry, [which] reinforces the conclusion that regulation of tobacco products under the Act was not intended by Congress."[27] The court's decision was stayed pending further appeal.

On November 10, 1998, in a 6-3 decision, the full appellate court rejected the Administration's request to reconsider the ruling.[28] The Justice Department filed a Petition for a Writ of Certiorari with the U.S. Supreme Court on January 19, 1999, requesting that the court review the Fourth Circuit ruling and find that the FDA hasfull statutory authority both to regulate tobacco products and to issue all the

[24] Id.

[25] The two youth access provisions were: (i) no sales to individuals under age 18; and (ii) photo ID required as a condition of sale for all individuals under age 27.

[26] Brown & Williamson Tobacco Corp. v. FDA, 153 F. 3d. 155 (4th Cir. 1998).

[27] Id. at 165.

[28] Brown & Williamson Tobacco Corp. v. FDA, 161 F.3d 764 (4th Cir. 1998).

provisions of the 1996 tobacco rule. The Supreme Court accepted the case and ultimately upheld the Fourth Circuit's decision.

U.S. Supreme Court (FDA v. Brown & Williamson Tobacco Corp.)

On March 21, 2000, the U.S. Supreme Court, in a 5-4 decision written by Justice Sandra Day O'Connor, affirmed the ruling of the appeals court that the FDA does not have the authority to regulate tobacco products as drug-delivery devices.[29] Although the majority opinion acknowledged the public health threat posed by tobacco use, the Court concluded that "Congress has clearly precluded the FDA from asserting jurisdiction to regulate tobacco products. Such authority is inconsistent with the intent that Congress has expressed in the [FFDCA's] overall regulatory scheme and in the tobacco-specific legislation that it has enacted subsequent to the [FFDCA]."[30]

In reaching its decision, the Court examined the FDA tobacco rule in light of the precedents that govern cases involving an agency's construction of a statute that it administers. As part of such a review, the Court must determine whether an agency's interpretation of its statute is entitled to deference and presents a reasonable or permissible construction of the law. Chevron U.S.A. v. NRDCh the leading case on judicial review of agency interpretations of statutes.[31] This case involved EPA's rules regulating emissions under the Clean Air Act. In Chevron, the Court enunciated a two-step test for judicial review of an agency's interpretation of its statute: (1) has Congress spoken directly to the precise question at issue? and; (2) if Congress has not done so and the statute is silent or ambiguous with respect to the specific issue, is the agency's answer based on a permissible construction of the statute?[32]

Under Chevron step one, if Congress has spoken directly to the question at issue, then Chevron deference is not due and the Court "must give effect to the unambiguously expressed intent of Congress."[33] In this case, the Court examined both the FFDCA and other tobacco-related statutes, ultimately concluding that Congress had clearly intended to preclude the FDA from regulating tobacco. As a result, the Court did not need to reach step two of Chevron. In reaching its decision, the Court relied on a number of factors. First, the Court found that, because tobacco is a dangerous product and because the FFDCA prohibits the

[29] FDA v. Brown & Williamson Tobacco Corp., 529 U.S. 120 (2000).
[30] Id. at 126.
[31] 467 U.S. 837 (1984).
[32] Id. at 842-43.

marketing of products that have not been found to be safe and effective, the statute would require the FDA to ban tobacco products if the agency did indeed have jurisdiction over such products. Such a ban, argued the Court, would plainly contradict the congressional intent reflected in the enactment of several pieces of legislation that clearlycontemplate the continued marketing of tobacco products.[34] Thus, the Court held that Congress had clearly "intended to exclude tobacco products from the FDA's jurisdiction."[35]

In addition, the Court found that the FDA had repeatedly denied that it had jurisdiction over tobacco and that Congress had repeatedly rejected bills that would have granted the agency such authority.[36] Instead, Congress had demonstrated its intent to create a distinct regulatory scheme for tobacco by enacting other tobacco-related regulatory statutes, such as the Federal Cigarette Labeling and Advertising Act and the Comprehensive Smokeless Tobacco Health Education Act.[37] The Court cited these tobacco-related statutes as additional evidence in support of its conclusion that Congress had intended to preclude the FDA from regulating tobacco.[38]

Writing in dissent, Justice Stephen Breyer argued that cigarettes and other tobacco products clearly fall within the plain meaning of the statutory definition of drugs and devices because such products are intended to affect the structure and function of the body. In addition, the dissent argued that the purpose of the FFDCA — to protect the public health — also supported the conclusion that the FDA was authorized to regulate tobacco products. For these reasons, the dissent would have upheld the FDA's jurisdiction over such products.[39]

The Supreme Court's decision clarifies that the FDA cannot assert jurisdiction over cigarettes and other tobacco products unless Congress enacts legislation to

---

[33] Id. at 843.

[34] FDA v. Brown & Williamson Tobacco Corp., 529 U.S. 120, 134-43 (2000). Examples of such tobacco-related legislation include the Federal Cigarette Labeling and Advertising Act (PL. 89-92, 15 U.S.C. §§ 1331 et seq.); the Public Health Cigarette Smoking Act of 1969 (PL. 91-222,15 U.S.C. §§ 1331 et seq.); the Comprehensive Smoking Education Act (PL. 98-474, 15 U.S.C. §§ 1331 et seq.); the Comprehensive Smokeless Tobacco Health Education Act of 1986 (PL. 99-252, 15 U.S.C. §§ 4401 et seq.); and the Alcohol, Drug Abuse, and Mental Health Administration Reorganization Act (PL. 102-321, § 202, 42 U.S.C. § 300x-26).

[35] FDA v. Brown & Williamson Tobacco Corp., 529 U.S. 120, 143 (2000).

[36] According to the tobacco companies, beginning in 1906 and as recently as 1993, Congress rejected any legislation designed to give the FDA jurisdiction over tobacco. Coyne Beahm, Inc. v. FDA, 966 F. Supp. 1374 (M.D.N.C. 1997) (No. 2:95CV00591), at 6-11 (First Amended Complaint for Declaratory and Injunctive Relief).

[37] These statutes, both of which are administered by the FTC, require health warnings on cigarette and smokeless tobacco packages and advertising, respectively.

[38] FDA v. Brown & Williamson Tobacco Corp., 529 U.S. 120, at 143-156.

[39] Id. at 161-64.

give the agency unambiguous statutory authority over such products. Lawmakers first drafted such language during the 105th Congress and included it in the comprehensive tobacco legislation that was introduced in an effort to implement the 1997 proposed national tobacco settlement.

1997 Proposed National Tobacco Settlement

On June 20, 1997, a group of state attorneys general announced that they had reached an agreement with the tobacco companies to settle the state tobacco lawsuits.[40] Forty-one states and Puerto Rico had sued the tobacco industry seeking to recover the costs, primarily Medicaid expenditures, of treating smoking-related diseases. Under the proposed national settlement, the industry agreed to pay $368.5 billion over the first 25 years, and $15 billion a year thereafter, to reimburse states for their tobacco-related medical costs and pay for tobacco-control programs to reduce tobacco use among teenagers. In addition to settling the state lawsuits, the proposed settlement would have terminated all pending class-action lawsuits and nicotine addiction claims, and provided the companies with immunity from such lawsuits in the future.

The proposed settlement incorporated all the provisions of the FDA tobacco rule and included additional restrictions on marketing and advertising, as well as new warning labels. It also proposed amending the FFDCA to classify tobacco products as Class II devices and give FDA the authority to reduce or eliminate harmful compounds added to tobacco products or found in smoke. A summary of the key provisions in the proposed national settlement is provided in the box on the next page.

Public health officials criticized the restrictions the proposed settlement would have placed on FDA's ability to regulate nicotine. For example, any proposal by the agency to reduce nicotine yields or eliminate other harmful ingredients in cigarettes would have required formal rulemaking with judicial review, instead of the informal, notice-and-comment rulemaking that is typically used by federal agencies to promulgate regulations. Formal rulemaking, which is seldom used today, involves trial-type hearings before an administrative judge, at which parties present evidence and conduct cross-examinations. It is a rigorous and lengthy process that places a considerable burden of proof on the agency.[41]

---

[40] The full text of the June 1997 proposed national tobacco settlement is available online at [http://www.stic.neu.edu/settlement/6-20-settle.htm].

[41] Most federal regulations are issued under the notice-and-comment procedure established by the Administrative Procedure Act (5 U.S.C. §§ 551 et seq.). The agency publishes a notice of

The FDA also would have been required to show that the proposed modification significantly reduced health risks and did not create a black market for unmodified products. Finally, the FDA would have to wait 12 years before proposing to eliminate nicotine from tobacco products.

The tobacco companies defended those restrictions on FDA's authority by claiming that they represented reasonable constraints on an agency that was seeking to eliminate its products.

Summary of Proposed National Tobacco Settlement (June 20, 1997)

FDA Regulation. Incorporated the following provisions of FDA's 1996 tobacco rule (21 CFR 897): prohibited sale of tobacco products to persons under age 18; required photo ID to verify age; limited advertising to which children are exposed to black-on-white, text-only format; prohibited the sale or distribution of promotional non-tobacco items such as hats and tee shirts; prohibited brand-name sponsorship of sporting and other events; required explicit warning labels. Extended the FDA's regulation by banning all vending machines and outdoor advertising, and prohibiting the use of human and cartoon images in advertising and packaging. Established strict regulatory requirements for reducing or eliminating nicotine from tobacco products, including formal rule making with judicial review and demonstrating that the modified product reduces health risks and does not create a black market for unmodified products.

Retailer Licensing. Set federal standards for licensing retailers who sell tobacco products. Retailers caught selling to minors would be fined or risk license revocation.

Industry Documents. Established a public depository of industry documents and created a three-judge arbitration panel to settle disputes over documents that are determined by the industry to be privileged against disclosure.

Non-Tobacco Ingredients. Required companies to disclose annually to FDA the amounts of all non-tobacco ingredients added to each brand, and to demonstrate that each ingredient is not harmful under the intended conditions of use.

---

proposed rulemaking in the Federal Register, solicits public comment, and incorporates in the final rule a concise statement about the rule's basis and purpose. Courts review such rules under the "arbitrary, capricious, and abuse of discretion" standard, generally upholding an agency's action if it is found to be rational, based on a consideration of the relevant factors, and within the scope of the authority designated to the agency by Congress. Formal rulemaking, by contrast, is a more rigorous and time-consuming process that tends to place a greater burden of proof on the agency promulgating the rule. Under the proposed national settlement, the FDA would have had to show "substantial evidence" in support of its cigarette performance standards, which is a more stringent standard than the arbitrary, capricious, and abuse of discretion standard.

Reduction of Youth Tobacco Use. Set targets for reducing the number of underage smokers: 30% reduction in five years; 60% in lOyears. Fined industry up to $2 billion ayear if targets are not met.

State Youth Access Laws. Required states to enforce their minimum-age-of-sale laws for tobacco products or risk losing settlement funds. The provisions expanded on those of the Synar Amendment.[a]

Environmental Tobacco Smoke. Restricted smoking in public buildings entered by 10 or more individuals at least once a week to separately ventilated smoking rooms. Exempted restaurants (except fast food), bars, private clubs, and prisons.

Industry Annual Payments. Required industry to pay $ 10 billion up front and annual payments beginning at $8.5 billioninthe firstyear, increasing to $15 billion in the fifth year, and remaining at $15 billion a year thereafter. Payments would be adjusted for inflation and volume of sales, and would be tax deductible. Total estimated payments over first 25 years = $368.5 billion.

Tobacco Control Programs and Research. Allocated funds to states to reimburse Medicaid programs and provide health insurance to uninsured children. Provided funds for tobacco cessation programs, counter advertising, biomedical research, FDA regulation, and federal, state, and local tobacco control programs.

Civil Liability. Terminated all pending state Medicaid and class-action lawsuits and prohibits such lawsuits in the future. Preserved the right of individuals to bring personal injury claims, but prohibited punitive damages in claims arising from past industry conduct. Limited the total damages paid by the industry in any one year to 33% of the annual payment.

a. The Synar Amendment (42 U.S.C. § 300x-26) requires states to enforce their laws prohibiting the sale of tobacco products to minors or risk losing 40% of their federal substance abuse block grant funding. States conduct annual random, unannounced inspections of retail outlets to ensure compliance with the laws. The Synar Amendment is administered by the Substance Abuse and Mental Health Services Administration, part of the Department of Health and Human Services.

McCain Tobacco Bill (105th Congress)

The proposed national settlement was presented to Congress as a blueprint for a comprehensive tobacco-control policy. Because the proposal included changes to the FFDCA and other federal statutes, it would have required congressional legislative action in order to take effect. Attempts by the 105th Congress to pass legislation to implement the settlement ended when the McCain bill (S. 1415) was defeated on a pair of procedural votes on June 17, 1998, after an extended floor debate. Following the demise of S. 1415, the major cigarette companies resumed negotiations with the states and, in November 1998, signed a contractual agreement — the Master Settlement Agreement, or MSA — to settle the state lawsuits.[42] The MSA did not address FDA's authority over tobacco products (see box below).

Tobacco Master Settlement Agreement (MSA)

On November 23, 1998, 46 states, the District of Columbia, and five U.S. territories signed a comprehensive agreement with the four major cigarette companies (Philip Morris Inc., R.J. Reynolds Tobacco Company, Brown & Williamson Tobacco Corp., and Lorillard Tobacco Company). The companies agreed to make annual payments to the states in perpetuity as reimbursement for past tobacco-related medical expenses.[a] The MSA required the companies to pay approximately $206 billion over the first 25 years. The four states that were not party to the MSA had reached earlier, individual settlements with the industry that called for payments totaling $40 billion over 25 years (MS, 7/3/1997; FL, 8/25/1997; TX, 1/16/1998; MN, 5/8/1998). Although it bore a superficial resemblance to the 1997 proposed national settlement, the MSA was considerably narrower in scope and did not require congressional action for its implementation. It settled only the state and local government lawsuits. Unlike the proposed national settlement, the MSA did not provide the industry with any legal protection from class-action lawsuits and claims brought by individuals, labor unions, and private health care insurers. While the companies agreed to some restrictions on cigarette advertising and marketing (similar to provisions in the FDA tobacco rule), the MSA lacked the broader tobacco-control initiatives that were included in the proposed national settlement and the McCain bill (e.g., retailer licensing, ingredient disclosure, youth tobacco use targets and penalties, and indoor smoking restrictions).

Of $61 million paid to the states by tobacco companies to date, states spent less than 8% on anti-smoking endeavors, according to a March 2007 article by the American Bar Association Journal.[b] Government Accountability Office figures indicate that states have spent even less on tobacco control, which it defines as efforts to include prevention, education, enforcement, and cessation services.[c] States have allocated 30% of their MSA payments to health care, including Medicaid, health insurance, and hospitals; 22.9% towards budget shortfalls; 7.1% to general purposes; 6% towards infrastructure; 5.5% to education; 5.4% to debt service on securitized funds; 3.5% on tobacco control; have not allocated 11.9%; and allocated 7.8% to other projects."[d]

a. Subsequently, Congress enacted PL. 106-31 in 2000, which allows the states to keep reimbursements they receive from third parties, such as tobacco companies, rather than

[42] The full text of the MSA is available on the website of the National Association of Attorneys General (NAAG), at [http://www.naag.org/issues/issue-tobacco.php]. NAAG is responsible for implementing and enforcing the MSA.

grant the federal government its share of any reimbursements of Medicaid funds. FY1999 Emergency Supplemental Appropriations Act § 3031. If a third party causes illness or injury to someone, and a state provides medical care for that illness or injury, as, for example, out of Medicaid funds, then the state may sue the third party for reimbursement of such funds. Because the federal government pays for at least 50% of each state's medical costs, by law the federalgovernment is entitled to its share of any non-tobacco company reimbursements of Medicaid funds that a state receives from a third party that caused an illness or injury on which Medicaid funds were expended. 42 U.S.C. § 1396b(d)(2)(B).

b. Mark Curriden, Up in Smoke, A.B.A. Journal, Mar. 2007, at 27.

c. Lisa Shames, Acting Director, Natural Resources and Environment, GAO, Testimony Before the Committee on Health, Education, labor, and Pensions, U.S. Senate (Feb. 27, 2007), Tobacco Settlement: States' Allocations of Payments from Tobacco Companies for Fiscal Years 2000 through 2005, at 14.

d. Shames, supra note c. Section 10908 of the Farm Security and Rural Investment Act of 2002mandates that GAO report on "all programs and activities that States have carried out using funds received under all phases of the Master Settlement Agreement of 1997." PL. 107-171.

Table 1, beginning on page 41, provides a summary of the major provisions of the McCain tobacco bill. Although the measure was intended to implement the proposed national settlement, it was tougher on the industry in several key respects. S. 1415 would have cost the companies $516 billion over the first 25 years, an amount significantly higher than the figure agreed to in the proposed settlement (i.e., $368.5 billion). It included stiffer financial penalties if the decline in underage tobacco use did not meet the reduction targets, and it also provided the industry with fewer legal protections than those negotiated in the June 1997 agreement.

The McCain bill also added a new Chapter LX to the FFDCA solely for the regulation of tobacco products. That language, which was provided by Senator Frist, drew extensively on the act's existing drug and device provisions in Chapter V, but with modifications.[43] By establishing new legal authority within the FFDCA for regulating tobacco products, the bill's sponsors sought to address the unique challenges tobacco products present and avoid the safety and effectiveness standard that applies to the regulation of drugs and devices. Under the new language, FDA would be required to demonstrate that any proposed tobacco

---

[43] The Frist language incorporated, with modifications, the following FFDCA drug and device provisions: adulterated drugs and devices (§ 501); misbranded drugs and devices (§ 502); device manufacturer registration (§ 510); performance standards (§ 514); premarket approval (§ 515); judicial review (§ 517); notification and recall (§ 518); records and reports (§ 519); general provisions respecting control of devices intended for human use (§ 520); preemption of state and local requirements (§ 521); and postmarket surveillance (§ 522).

regulation was appropriate for the protection of public health. Such a determination would involve a consideration of the risks and benefits to the population as a whole.

The tobacco companies opposed S. 1415 and launched a $40 million advertising campaign that helped defeat it. They portrayed the legislation as nothing more than a massive tax increase to pay for new government spending. During the Senate floor debate, which stretched over four weeks (May 18-June 17,1998), lawmakers focused on where the bill's revenues should go, how to compensate tobacco growers, and whether to limit the fees of private attorneys who were retained by the states. Amendments were added to the bill to eliminate the so-called marriage income tax penalty, boost funding for anti-drug programs, and cap attorneys' fees. There was no debate on the bill's FDA provisions.

Public health officials supported many of the McCain bill's tobacco-control provisions, but were critical of the measure's FDA provisions. They feared that theagency's attempts to implement the new law would be blocked at every turn by lengthy legal challenges from the industry. Instead, they sided with the FDA's arguments for asserting jurisdiction under existing law (i.e., FFDCA's Chapter V device provisions). In its rulemaking the agency concluded that the device provisions, which have been interpreted in case law, regulation, and agency practice for over two decades, have established a comprehensive regulatory scheme that is appropriate for regulating tobacco products.

Several other comprehensive tobacco bills were introduced in the 105th Congress, though none of them saw any legislative activity.[44] The bills, which were supported by the public health community and opposed by the industry, would have given FDA explicit authority to regulate tobacco products under the FFDCA's Chapter V drug and device provisions. In each case, the legislation amended the act's definitions of drugs and devices to include nicotine and tobacco products, respectively, and authorized the agency to regulate tobacco products using a standard of protecting the public health. By avoiding having to regulate tobacco products based on safety and effectiveness, the agency would have been able to keep such unhealthful products on the market. For more details, see CRS Report 98-6, Tobacco Legislation in the 105th Congress.

[44] S. 1492 (Kennedy); S. 1530 (Hatch); S. 1638 (Conrad); S. 1889 (Harkin); H.R. 3028 (DeLauro); H.R. 3474 (Fazio); H.R. 3868 (Hansen).

FDA Tobacco Legislation Since the 107th Congress

This section of the report includes a brief description of the tobacco legislation introduced in the 107th Congress (2001-2002) in the wake of the Supreme Court decision, followed by a summary of tobacco legislation introduced in the 108th to the 110th Congresses and some analysis of H.R. 1108/S. 625. Because some of the legislation introduced during these sessions was drafted, at least in part, in response to Philip Morris's new position on FDA tobacco regulation, the section begins by comparing Philip Morris's position on FDA tobacco regulation with that of the leading anti-tobacco organizations. The President's Cancer Panel has recommended granting the FDA regulatory authority over tobacco,[45] as has the Institute of Medicine.[46] However, the Bush administration and the FDA Commissioner, Andrew von Eschenbach, have indicated concerns regarding the legislation, specifically that the bill would be "creating a false impression that regulated tobacco products weresafe,"[47] and "that this will actually encourage individuals to smoke more rather than less."[48]

Competing Views on FDA Regulatory Authority

Philip Morris U.S.A. In March 2001, Philip Morris, the nation's leading cigarette company with about 51% of the U.S. market, issued a white paper in support of legislation giving FDA authority to regulate cigarettes.[49] The company explained that its support for such legislation did not signal a reversal of its earlier opposition to the FDA's attempt to regulate cigarettes as restricted medical devices. Philip Morris opposed the FDA rule on the grounds that it would have left the agency with no choice but to ban the sale of cigarettes. The company argued that cigarettes simply cannot be found to be safe and effective as required

---

45 President's Cancer Panel, 2006-2007 Annual Report, Promoting Healthy Lifestyles: Policy, Program, and Personal Recommendations for Reducing Cancer Risk, at xi, xvii, 7475, 106, 113 [http://deainfo.nci.nih.gov/ADVISORY/pcp/pcp07rpt/pcp07rpt.pdf].

46 Institute of Medicine, Report Brief: Ending the Tobacco Problem: A Blueprint for the Nation, at 6 (May 2007), [http://www.iom.edu/Object.File/Master/43/183/Tobacco%20 report%20brief%20general.pdf].

47 Stephanie Saul, Bill to Regulate Tobacco as a Drug Is Approved by a House Committee, N.Y. Times, April 3, 2008, at C3.

48 H.R. 1108, Family Smoking Prevention and Tobacco Control Act, Hearing Before the Subcomm. on Health of the H. Comm. on Energy and Commerce, 110th Cong. (October 3, 2007) (written statement of Andrew C. von Eschenbach, Commissioner of Food and Drugs, FDA), [http://www.fda.gov/ola/2007/tobacco100307.html].

49 The Philip Morris white paper on FDA tobacco regulation is available online at [http://www.pmusa.com/ policies_practices/legislation_regulation/fda_tobacco.asp].

under the FFDCA's existing drug and device provisions, a position with which the Supreme Court agreed in FDA v. Brown & Williamson.

In the white paper, Philip Morris announced its support for legislation giving FDA new legal authority to regulate cigarettes, not as drugs or medical devices but in a manner that reflects the "unique challenges that cigarettes present." Such regulation, said the company, "would provide greater consistency in tobacco policy, more predictability for the tobacco industry, and an effective way to address issues that are of concern.... These issues include youth smoking; ingredient and [smoke] constituent testing and disclosure; content of health warning on cigarette packages and in advertisements; use of brand descriptors such as "light" and "ultra light"; good manufacturing practices for cigarettes; and standards for defining, and for the responsible marketing of any reduced risk or reduced exposure cigarettes."

Philip Morris set out in the white paper some fundamental principles for FDA tobacco legislation:

- Tobacco regulation should reflect the unique health, social and economic issues associated with such products. Cigarettes should be regulated as cigarettes, not as a medical device.
- Regulation should not equal prohibition. Adults should be able to make their own decision whether to smoke. The government should continue to inform the public about the dangers of tobacco products and discourage their consumption, but should not restrict an adult's ability to make a decision about smoking.
- Regulation should build on the framework of the MSA in working to prevent youth smoking.
- FDA should require that ingredients added by the manufacturers do not increase the inherent risks or addictiveness of smoking. The agency should have the authority to impose mandatory design changes to cigarettes to help reduce harm, provided the changes do not significantly diminish adult smokers' enjoyment of the product.
- Regulation should define reduced exposure and reduced risk products and establish guidelines for communications about such products in a way that is consistent and accurate and does not encourage smoking or discourage quitting.
- FDA should continue to address the broad issues of disclosure (e.g., the content of warning labels, information about ingredients and smoke constituents) so that adults smokers remain informed about health risks.

The overarching concern for Philip Morris was that any new legislation must recognize cigarettes as legal products and respect the decision of adults to smoke. The company has indicated that it opposes any proposals that would give FDA the authority to ban cigarettes outright or to achieve a de facto prohibition by imposing ever-lower tar and nicotine yields that would render the product unpalatable to adult smokers. Such product changes, argued the company, would drive smokers towards illicit, unregulated products, where there are no standards for ingredients or tar and nicotine levels. Interestingly, FDA used a similar line of reasoning in developing the tobacco rule when it concluded that banning tobacco products under the FFDCA's drug and device provisions was not a realistic option. The agency reasoned that a ban on cigarettes would encourage cigarette smuggling and the development of a black market supplying smokers with unregulated and potentially more dangerous products.

On February 15,2007, in a letter to Senators Kennedy and Cornyn, a senior vice president of Altria, Philip Morris's parent corporation, endorsed S. 625 on the companies' behalf.[50] The letter highlighted "important features" of the bill, some of which restated prior concerns above, and which included the statement that "[tjhebill would not, however, change the Supreme Court's rulings regarding the product liability implications of compliance with warning requirements."[51] The letter is likely referring to the 1992 U.S. Supreme Court case Cipollone v. Liggett Group, Lnc.[52] For an explanation of the Court's decision in this case, see pages 32 to 34.

Other Tobacco Companies

While Philip Morris has been actively lobbying for FDA tobacco legislation, the other major cigarette companies — R. J. Reynolds (which merged with Brown & Williamson in July 2004) and Lorillard — have criticized the various legislative proposals. Like Philip Morris, Lorillard supports additional regulation of tobacco manufacturers and tobacco products, but emphasizes that the FDA may "ultimately move to ban the conventional cigaretteproduct" and that some legislation may "allow the FDA to alter what occurs naturally in the [tobacco] leaf."[53] Lorillard believes that federal legislation "must advocate the research and

---

[50] Letter from Steven C. Parrish, Senior Vice President, Corporate Affairs, Altria Group, Inc., to SenatorsEdward M. Kennedy and John Cornyn (February 15, 2007), [http://www.altria.com/download/pdf/ SCP_FDA_Endorsement_Senate.pdf].

[51] Id.

[52] 505 U.S. 504 (1992).

[53] Lorillard Tobacco Company [http://www.lorillard.com/index.php?id=6].

oversee the development of potentially reduced exposure products" and "should codify the marketing and advertising restrictions already agreed to" in the MSA.[54] R.J. Reynolds would support additional "reasonable" regulation of tobacco products provided that tobacco remains legal and that any new regulation preserves the rights of adults to choose and purchase a wide range of "consumer-acceptable" cigarettes brands.[55] But they also stress the importance of maintaining a level playing field upon which manufacturers can compete for the business of adult smokers. This final point appears to lie at the heart of their opposition to the proposed legislation. R.J. Reynolds and Lorillard, which together accounted for approximately 38% of the U. S. cigarette market in 2003,[56] fear that sweeping new regulation of their products, including tight restrictions on marketing, will be to Philip Morris's advantage, allowing the nation's number one cigarette manufacturer to lock in its leading market share. They worry that new restrictions on advertising would force consumers to rely on brand recognition and product placement, which would give industry-leader Philip Morris an advantage.[57]

Campaign for Tobacco-Free Kids

Working in partnership with the nation's leading anti-tobacco organizations, including the American Lung Association, the American Cancer Society, and the American Heart Association, the Campaign for Tobacco-Free Kids developed a set of core elements that it believes must be incorporated in legislation giving FDA authority to regulate tobacco products.[58] While the Campaign and Philip Morris appear to be in general agreement on several areas over which FDA should be granted authority (e.g., youth access and marketing, ingredient testing and disclosure, good manufacturing practice, and reduced risk products), they fundamentally disagree on whether any limitations should be placed on that authority. Speaking for the anti-tobacco community at large, the Campaign argues

[54] Id.

[55] R.J. Reynolds Tobacco Company, Our Position on Further Federal Regulation, [http://www.rjrt.com/legal/ fedRegPo sition.asp].

[56] R.J. Reynolds has a U.S. market share of approximately 30%. R.J. Reynolds Tobacco Company Factbook, [http://www.rjrt.com/company/profileFactBook.asp]. Lorillard's market share has been estimated at 8%. Brian Louis, RJR Demotes Winston Brand, Winston-Salem Journal, September 19, 2003.

[57] For a discussion of company positions on FDA regulation and government regulation, visit each company's website: R. J. Reynolds Tobacco Company [http://www.rjrt.com/ legal/fedFDA.asp]; Lorillard Tobacco Company [http://www.lorillard.com/index.php?id=6].

[58] The Campaign summarizes elements of H.R. 1108/S. 625 that address "issues that have been considered critical" in any legislation giving FDA authority to regulate tobacco products. [http://tobaccofreekids.org/research/ factsheets/pdf/0181.pdf].

that FDA should be granted broad and unrestricted regulatory authority to take those actions it deems necessary to protect the public health. For example, the Campaign points to "deceptive marketing" practices, the addictivenature of tobacco products, and "unsubstantiated health claims made for new and low tar products" as evidence of the need for FDA regulatory authority.[59]

Institute of Medicine (IOM)

In May 2007, the Institute of Medicine published Ending the Tobacco Problem: A Blueprint for the Nation, the report of its study of tobacco use in the United States, which was funded by the American Legacy Foundation.[60] The IOM reported that in order to achieve long-lasting changes in tobacco use, Congress and other policymakers would need to grant FDA or another regulatory agency broad authority over the manufacture, distribution, marketing and use of tobacco products. The IOM specifically recommended that:

- Tobacco manufacturers be required to disclose all chemical compounds found in both their product and the product's smoke, by quantity; disclose to the public the content and delivery of nicotine, based on standards established by the FDA or other regulatory agency; and disclose to the public research on their product, as well as behavioral aspects of its use.
- Currently mandated federal health warnings be strengthened to promote greater understanding of the health risks of tobacco use and to discourage consumption. Congress should strengthen the federally mandated warning labels for tobacco products and delegate authority to the FDA to update and revise these warning on a regular basis.
- Congress and state legislatures enact legislation regulating the retail point of sale of tobacco products. Congress should empower FDA to restrict retail outlets in order to limit access and facilitate regulation of the retail environment, and thereby protect the public health.

The IOM also recommended that the federal government establish the necessary capacity for long-term tobacco policy development.

---

[59] Hearing on H.R. 1108, Family Smoking Prevention and Tobacco Control Act Before the H. Subcomm. on Health of the H. Comm. on Energy and Commerce, 110th Cong. (October 3, 2007) (statement of William V. Corr, Executive Director, Campaign for Tobacco Free Kids), at 6 [http://energycommerce.house.gov/cmte_mtgs/ 110-he-hrg.100307.Corr-testimony.pdf].

[60] Institute of Medicine, Ending the Tobacco Problem: A Blueprint for the Nation, The National Academies Press, May 2007, at [http://www.iom.edu/CMS/3793/20076/43179. aspx].

107th Congress

Philip Morris released its white paper early in the 107th Congress. Several FDA tobacco bills were introduced in that Congress, none of which saw any legislative action. Four bills (i.e., S. 190 (Frist), S. 2626 (Kennedy), S. 2764 (Miller), and H.R. 2180 (Tom Davis)) adopted the same approach as the McCain legislation. They would have created a new FFDCA Chapter IX solely for the regulation of tobacco products. Senator Kennedy's bill (S. 2626) was almost identical to the FDA provisions in the McCain bill. The three other bills included many of the same provisions. However, they contained a few small but significant changes that were intended to address industry concerns over the extent of FDA's regulatory control. For example, all three measures specified that FDA could not compel the industry to change the composition of its products in ways that would render them "unacceptable for adult consumption." They also required the agency to show that any proposal to restrict the sale, distribution, advertising, and promotion of tobacco products was based on a determination that such regulation "would be appropriate for the prevention of, or decrease in, the use of tobacco products by children...." Finally, all three measures reserved for Congress — not FDA — the authority to eliminate nicotine or ban tobacco products.

In addition to giving FDA new regulatory authority over tobacco products, H.R. 2180 also contained restrictions on youth access, advertising, and marketing that were broadly similar to those included in the McCain bill. The provisions in H.R. 2180 were subsequently incorporated into Representative Mclntyre's bill (H.R. 3940) to eliminate tobacco quotas and the price support loan program and compensate quota owners and active growers. S. 2764 also contained substantially similar buyout provisions.

The three remaining FDA tobacco bills introduced in the 107th Congress (i.e., S. 247 (Harkin), H.R. 1044 (Waxman), and H.R. 1097 (Ganske)), rather than creating new legal authority for regulating tobacco products, would have given FDA the authority to regulate tobacco products as drug-delivery devices under Chapter V of the FFDCA. This approach was favored by some public health advocates, but strongly opposed by the industry. As with the earlier versions introduced during the 105th Congress, each of these bills merely amended the definitions of drugs and devices to include nicotine and tobacco products, respectively, and specified that tobacco regulation would be based on a general standard of protecting the public health. Additionally, the three measures would have made effective all the provisions of the 1996 FDA tobacco rule.

108th Congress

At the beginning of the 108th Congress, Representatives Mclntyre and Tom Davis reintroduced their tobacco legislation (H.R. 140). The measure combined a buyout for quota owners and active growers with FDA regulatory authority. H.R. 140 was supported by Philip Morris but opposed by the public health community. In the Senate, negotiations among members of the Committee on Health, Education, Labor, and Pension (HELP) to draft a compromise bill that had the support of both sides came to a standstill in October 2003. Anti-smoking advocates and their congressional supporters criticized the draft legislation for failing to give FDA sufficient authority to protect public health.

Negotiations resumed in early 2004 and on May 20 Senators DeWine and Kennedy and Representatives Tom Davis and Henry Waxman introduced the Family Smoking Prevention and Tobacco Control Act (S. 2461, H.R. 4433). Both Philip Morris and the Campaign for Tobacco-Free Kids announced their "enthusiastic" support for the legislation. On July 15, Senator DeWine introduced the text of S. 2461 as an amendment to the American Jobs Creation Act of 2004 (H.R. 4520, P.L. 108-357), which was under consideration on the Senator floor. The amendment passed by a vote of 78-15. However, during the conference on H.R. 4520, the House conferees on October 6 rejected the DeWine amendment. Following its rejection by the conference committee, Senators DeWine and Kennedy reintroduced the legislation with a new bill number (S. 2974) on October 10. The measure was passed on the Senate floor that same day without amendment by unanimous consent. No further action was taken by either chamber.

109th Congress

Senators DeWine and Kennedy and Representatives Davis and Waxman reintroduced the Family Smoking Prevention and Tobacco Control Act on March 17, 2005. There was no legislative action taken on the legislation during the 109th Congress.

110th Congress

Representatives Waxman and Davis and Senators Kennedy and Cornyn introduced H.R. 1108 and S. 625, respectively, onFebruary 15, 2007. As introduced the legislation was nearly identical to H.R. 4433 and S. 2461 of the

108th Congress. On August 1, 2007, the Senate HELP Committee adopted a handful of amendments to S. 625 and approved the measure (as amended) by a vote of 13-8. On April 2, 2008, the House Energy and Commerce Committee took up a manager's amendment to H.R. 1108, which included several provisions intended to address the concerns of various stakeholder groups. The Committee then adopted three additional amendments before approving the bill (as amended) by a vote of 38-12. While the two bills, as reported, remain broadly similar, there are a number of significant differences between them. Table 2, beginning on page 45, summarizes the provisions in S. 625 and indicates key differences in H.R. 1108.

Issues

H.R. 1108/S. 625 represents an attempt to balance the competing interests of Philip Morris and leading anti-tobacco groups. The legislation would grant FDA the authority to:

- restrict tobacco advertising and promotions, especially to children;
- stop illegal sales of tobacco products to children;
- develop performance standards that require changes in the composition and design of tobacco products, such as the reduction or elimination of harmful chemicals;
- prohibit claims about reduced-risk and reduced-exposure tobacco products that are not scientifically substantiated or that would discourage current tobacco users from quitting or encourage new users to start;
- prohibit terms such as "light," "mild," or "low tar" that can mislead consumers into believing that certain products are safer than others;
- require larger and more explicit health warnings on tobacco products.

At the same time, H.R. 1108/S. 625 explicitly states that one of its purposes is "to continue to permit the sale of tobacco products to adults in conjunction with measures to ensure that they are not sold or accessible to underage purchasers." The legislation states that FDA may not prohibit the sale of tobacco products to individuals age 18 and over. However, state laws with a minimum age of sale of tobacco products greater than 18 years of age (for example, age 19) would not appear to be preempted by the bills. Moreover, it provides that only Congress may impose a new standard that would ban tobacco products or require the "reduction of nicotine yields of a tobacco product to zero." The following provides more discussion and analysis of these and other provisions in the bills.

Restrictions on Advertising and Promotion; First Amendment Issues

H.R. 1108/S. 625 would give FDA broad authority to regulate tobacco product marketing if it determined that such regulation was appropriate to protect the public health. The agency would be required to make that determination based on a consideration of the "risks and benefits to the population as a whole," including whether the agency's actions would discourage current users from quitting or encourage others to start using tobacco products.[61]

It is helpful to review briefly the U. S. Supreme Court's decisions on government regulation of advertising and other forms of commercial speech.[62] In Central Hudson Gas & Electric Corp. v. Public Service Commission (1980), the Court established a four-part test for deciding the constitutionality of commercial speech regulation.[63] First, in order to be protected by the First Amendment, the commercial speech must concern lawful activity and not be false or misleading. Second, the government must demonstrate that by restricting such speech, it is seeking to further a substantial government interest. Third, the restrictions must directly advance that interest. Fourth, there has to be a reasonable fit between the type of restrictions imposed andthe government's objectives — in other words the regulation cannot be "more extensive than is necessary to service that interest."[64]

The U.S. Supreme Court has issued a series of decisions striking down government restrictions on commercial speech, including tobacco product

[61] H.R. 1108, § 102 (to be codified at § 906(d)(1)). In the past, Philip Morris criticized that approach and preferred the language of H.R. 140 in the 108th Congress, which would have permitted FDA to regulate tobacco advertising and promotion based on a determination that such regulation was "appropriate for the prevention of, or decrease in, the use of tobacco products by [minors]." Anti-tobacco groups believed that such a standard would make it virtually impossible for FDA to act. They argued that because the industry denied that any of its advertising is directed at children, it would have challenged every regulatory proposal by the agency. Philip Morris defended the language, arguing that it was simply a recognition of the fact that the First Amendment, as currently interpreted by the U.S. Supreme Court, "prevents the FDA from prohibiting advertising directed at adults." The company contended that giving the agency broader authority to regulate the marketing of its products would be inefficient because it would have encouraged FDA to develop regulations that would never survive a constitutional challenge.

[62] For more information on the First Amendment and commercial speech, see CRS Report 95-815A, Freedom of Speech and Press: Exceptions to the First Amendment, by Henry Cohen.

[63] 447 U.S. 557 (1980).

[64] 447 U.S. at 566.

advertising.[65] In Lorillard Tobacco Co. v. Reilly (2001), the Court found a number of Massachusetts state regulations restricting outdoor and point-of-sale advertising for cigars and smokeless tobacco products to be unconstitutional.[66] The Court determined that the regulations restricted speech more than was reasonable to advance the state's interest in reducing underage (i.e., illegal) use of tobacco products and, thus, failed to meet the fourth part of the Central Hudson test. Banning all outdoor tobacco advertisements within 1,000 feet of a school or playground, in conjunction with other zoning restrictions, argued the Court, "would constitute a nearly complete ban on the communication of truthful information about smokeless tobacco and cigars to adult consumers."[67] The Court found that the restrictions on outdoor advertising of cigars and smokeless tobacco were overbroad in that they prohibited advertising "in a substantial portion of the major metropolitan areas of Massachusetts," included oral communications, and imposed burdens on retailers with limited advertising budgets.[68] The Court also upheld challenges by smokeless tobacco and cigar companies to the outdoor advertising restrictions on the grounds that adults have a right to information and the tobacco industry has a right to communicate truthful speech on legal products.[69]

In developing the 1996 tobacco rule, which H.R. 1108/S.625 would require the Secretary of Health and Human Services (HHS) to publish as a final rule within 30 days (S. 625) or 180 days (H.R. 1108) after enactment, FDA created a set of advertising restrictions aimed at reducing underage smoking and smokeless tobacco use that it hoped would withstand a constitutional challenge. Whether the FDA rule would have passed the Central Hudson test remains unclear. In FDA v. Brown & Williamson, the Supreme Court confined itself to a review of the agency's interpretation of its authority under the FFDCA. The Court did not address the constitutionality of the rule's marketing restrictions. The FDA's 1996 rule would have limited advertisements in publications with a significant teen audience to black text on a white background.[70] The 1996 rule also included a ban

[65] Ronald Beyer et al., "Tobacco Advertising in the United States: A Proposal for a Constitutionally Acceptable Form of Regulation," Journal of the American Medical Association, vol. 287, no. 22 (June 2002), pp. 2990-95.
[66] 533 U.S. 525 (2001).
[61] Id. at 562.
[68] Id. at 562, 564-65.
[69] Id. at 564.
[70] If H.R. 1108/S. 625 pass and the FDA's 1996 final rule becomes law, 21 C.F.R. § 897.32 will permit labeling or advertising for cigarettes or smokeless tobacco with "only black text on a white background," except in facilities "where vending machines and self-service displays are permitted . . . provided that the advertising is not visible from outside the facility and that it is affixed to a wall or fixture in the facility" or in an adult publication. Regulations Restricting the

on outdooradvertising within 1,000 feet of a school or playground. As noted, in Lorillard, the Court found a similar provision in the Massachusetts regulations unconstitutional.

At the markup of H.R. 1108 in the House Committee on Energy and Commerce, Representatives Waxman, Buyer, and Dingell debated whether the Court's holding in Lorillard would impact the 1996 rule's restriction on advertisements within 1,000 feet of a school or playground, which H.R. 1108 would require to be published in the Federal Register as a final rule.[71] The committee report on H.R. 1108 similarly addresses this debate in the section-by-section analysis and the dissenting views.[72] Analyzing this restriction in the context of Central Hudson, it does not appear that the 1996 rule's restriction on advertisements within 1,000 feet of a school or playground would survive the fourth step of the Central Hudson test — that the regulation cannot be "more extensive than is necessary" to serve the substantial government interest.[73] In Lorillard, the Court stated that "[t]he broad sweep of the regulations indicates that the Attorney General did not 'carefully calculate the costs and benefits associated with the burden on speech imposed' by the regulations."[74] The Supreme Court further explained that a "careful calculation of the costs of a speech regulation does not mean that a State must demonstrate that there is no incursion on legitimate speech interests, but a speech regulation cannot unduly impinge on the speaker's ability to propose a commercial transaction and the adult listener's opportunity to obtain information about products."[75]

First, the Court noted that "the Attorney General did not seem to consider the impact of the 1,000 foot restriction on commercial speech in major metropolitan areas."[76] Rather, the Attorney General imposed a 1,000 foot restriction that was identical to the FDA's restriction in the 1996 rule. The Court noted that suppression of speech or limits on speech tend to be case-specific. However, "the FDA'sregulations would have had widely disparate effects nationwide.... The

Sale and Distribution of Cigarettes and Smokeless Tobacco to Protect Children and Adolescents, 61 FR 44617 (August 28, 1996). An adult publication would be defined under 21 C.F.R. § 897.32(a)(2) as a newspaper, magazine, periodical, or other publication: (I) Whose readers younger than 18 years of age constitute 15 percent or less of the total readership as measured by competent and reliable survey evidence and (ii) That is read by fewer than 2 million persons younger than 18 years of age as measured by competent and reliable survey evidence.

61 Fed. Reg. 44617.

[71] H.R. 1108, § 102(a).

[72] H.Rept. 110-762, at 72-73, 159 (2008).

[73] 447 U.S. at 566.

[74] Id. at 561 (quoting Cincinnati v. Discovery Network, Inc., 507 U. S. 410, 417 (1993)).

[75] Id. at 565-66.

uniformly broad sweep of the geographical limitation demonstrates a lack of tailoring."[77] In the FDA's final 1996 rule, the agency took note of comments that focused on the impact of the rule in major metropolitan areas, including a survey that "showed that outdoor tobacco advertising would be prohibited in 94 percent and 78 percent of the respective land mass of Manhattan and Boston under the [1,000 foot] proposal."[78] However, the FDA attributed "the possibility that its restrictions effectively outlaw outdoor advertising in most urban areas" to population density in cities.[79] The agency then stated that its intent in establishing the 1,000 foot restriction was "to restrict the accessible and intrusive communications of information about cigarettes and smokeless tobacco to children and adolescents at school and at play."[80] The rule explained that the FDA "considered the cost of its [1,000 foot] restriction but conclude[d] that a narrower restriction would not adequately advance its purpose of protecting young people from unavoidable advertising."[81] The Lorillard Court's declaration that a 87 to 91 percent ban on tobacco advertising "would constitute nearly a complete ban on the communication of truthful information about smokeless tobacco and cigars to adult consumers" and the Court's statement that the 1,000 foot restrictions' "breadth and scope ... [did] not demonstrate a careful calculation of the speech interests involved,"appear to indicate that Court would strike the 1,000 foot restriction if the 1996 final rule became effective.[82]

Second, the Court stated that tailored restrictions on tobacco advertising and promotion "would involve targeting those practices [that appeal to children] while permitting others."[83] The FDA stated in its responses to comments on the rulemaking:

> The prohibition on outdoor advertising within 1,000 feet of schools and playgrounds is designed to address a different problem. The concern is not the appeal of the advertising. If the problem were only appeal, the 1,000 foot restriction would not be necessary because the text-only requirement would eliminate this concern. The concern is the nature of the billboards themselves. Billboards near schools and playgrounds ensure that children are exposed to their messages for a prolonged period of time.[84]

[76] Id. at 562.
[77] Id. at 563.
[78] 61 Fed. Reg. 44506.
[79] Id.
[80] Id.
[81] Id.
[82] 447 U.S. at 562.
[83] Id. at 563.
[84] 61 Fed. Reg. 44506.

Therefore, it does not seem likely that the Supreme Court would uphold the 1,000 foot restriction if, as the agency stated, it was not meant to target practices that appeal to children. Based on the Court's discussion in Lorillard, it does not appear likely that the 1996 FDA final rule's 1,000 foot restriction would survive a Central Hudsonanalysis.[85] However, as specified in section 102(a)(2) of H.R. 1108/S. 625 for other parts of the 1996 final rule, which the legislation would require to be published as a final rule 180 days after enactment, Congress could exclude the 1,000 foot restriction.

Some public health law experts believe that the Supreme Court in its decisions on the regulation of commercial speech has left public health authorities with little room to craft tobacco advertising restrictions that meet both the third (effectiveness) and fourth (extensiveness) parts of the Central Hudson test.[86] On the one hand, tobacco advertising restrictions that are narrowly tailored may not provide clear evidence of effectiveness, thus failing the third part of Central Hudson test. On the other hand, more sweeping (and potentially effective) restrictions may be viewed as too extensive and not reasonably related to the government's asserted interest, thus failing the fourth part of the Central Hudson test.

In the event that the advertising restrictions are challenged, H.R. 1108/S. 625 contain severability clauses that states:

> If any provision of this Act, the amendments made by this Act, or the application of any provision of this Act to any person or circumstance is held to be invalid, the remainder of this Act, the amendments made by this Act, and the application of the provisions of this Act to any other person or circumstance shall not be affected and shall continue to be enforced to the fullest extent possible.[87]

Product Design and Composition

H.R. 1108/S 625 would not permit cigarettes to contain any additive that is a "characterizing flavor" of the product or the smoke, other than tobacco or menthol.[88] The legislation would give FDA the authority to develop product standards to reduce nicotine, reduce or eliminate other harmful constituents, or

---

85 61 Fed. Reg. 44507-08.

86 Beyer et al., supra n. 65.

87 H.R. 1108, 110th Cong. § 5 (2007); S. 625, 100th Cong. § 5 (2007).

88 R.J. Reynolds reached an agreement with several states attorneys general regarding the adult-only marketing and sale of flavored cigarettes named after a fruit, candy, or alcoholic beverage. Press Release, R.J. Reynolds Tobacco Company, Attorneys General Agree on Flavored Cigarette Marketing Guidelines, October 11, 2006, [http://www.rjrt.com/newsroom/resourcesRJRTview.asp?postID=1178].

otherwise modify the composition and testing of tobacco products, if it determined that such regulation was appropriate to protect the public health. Once again, FDA would be required to make that determination based on a consideration of the risks and benefits to the population as a whole, which is the approach favored by public health officials. Unlike some of the previous FDA tobacco bills, there is nothing in H.R. 1108/S. 625 to prevent the agency from requiring changes in the composition of tobacco products that would render them "unacceptable for adult consumption." Placing that restriction on FDA's ability to modify tobacco products had been a key requirement for the industry.

Critics of the idea of reduced nicotine levels, including FDA Commissioner Andrew von Eschenbach, argue that "if the FDA ordered a cut in nicotine levels, smokers would alter their smoking habits in order to maintain their current levels ofthe addictive substance."[89] Von Eschenbach said that such a decision could "ma[k]e the public health radically worse."[90] On the other hand, supporters say that smokers may not compensate for reduced nicotine levels by inhaling deeper or smoking more frequently. Rather, reduced nicotine levels may help smokers quit altogether.[91]

The authority to set product standards would give FDA an important tool for modifying tobacco products already on the market so as to make them less harmful. However, developing such standards may be a long and difficult process. More than 4,000 chemical compounds have been identified in tobacco smoke, including about 60 known carcinogens. Researchers still know relatively little about the precise mechanisms by which individual compounds and groups of related compounds contribute to the overall health risks of smoking. It may take years to collect the data necessary to demonstrate that the reduction or elimination of a particular tobacco product constituent will lead to an improvement in public health.

As part of the standard-setting process, FDA would also be required to consider whether a proposed standard might lead to a "significant demand for contraband products and other tobacco products that do not meet the requirements of the [legislation]" Until more is learned about the nature of nicotine addiction, that requirement may pose a significant challenge to any proposed reduction in nicotine yield.

H.R. 1108/S. 625 does not permit FDA to ban tobacco products, or to require the reduction of nicotine yields to zero. The authority to take those specific actions is reserved for Congress. As discussed earlier, the industry has argued

89 Lower Nicotine Levels in Cigarettes Could Backfire: FDA Chief, Wash. Post, March 6, 2007.
90 Id.
91 Id.

strenuously in favor of placing such restrictions on FDA's regulatory authority. Companies are fearful that the agency, left unchecked, could achieve a de facto ban by eliminating nicotine and making tobacco products unacceptable to adults. The public health community maintains that FDA should have unrestricted authority to take whatever actions it feels are necessary to protect public health.

Reduced Risk Products

Both the tobacco industry and the public health community are eager to establish a regulatory scheme for "reduced-risk" tobacco products. In recent years Philip Morris and the other leading cigarette companies have test marketed a variety of products that are potentially less harmful to the individual user than traditional tobacco products. They include cigarettes made using genetically modified tobacco, and cigarette-like products that deliver nicotine using a combustion process that involves lower temperatures and a more controlled burn. The companies want FDA's approval to market these products without fear of the agency taking regulatory action against them. FDA has in the past assertedjurisdiction when cigarette manufacturers have expressly promoted their products as beneficial to health.[92]

Public health advocates insist that FDA be given the authority not just to assess industry claims that a reduced-risk product is less harmful to the individual user under normal conditions of use, but also to weigh the risks and benefits to the wider population. They are concerned about recent efforts by the smokeless tobacco companies to market oral snuff and chewing tobacco as a safer alternative to smoking. The companies see the growing anti-smoking sentiment in the country and the spread of indoor (and outdoor) smoking restrictions as an opportunity to market their products to smokers who have trouble finding somewhere to smoke and who are considering alternative sources of nicotine. Epidemiological studies indicate that compared to smoking cigarettes, using smokeless tobacco products exposes an individual to less overall risk from a narrower range of diseases. But public health experts worry that promoting smokeless tobacco as a safer alternative to smoking will undermine efforts both to discourage youngsters from using smokeless tobacco and to encourage adult

[92] The FFDCA's definition of drug includes "articles intended foruse in the diagnosis, cure, mitigation, treatment, or prevention of disease...." (§ 201(g)(1)(B)) During the 1950s, the agency took regulatory action against cigarettes advertised as effective in preventing respiratory and other diseases and cigarettes promoted as weight-reduction aids. Note: The FDA regulates several nicotine replacement therapies to help tobacco users quit. These products include nicotine gum, transdermal nicotine patches, nicotine inhalers, and nicotine nasal spray.

smokers to give up tobacco products altogether. As a consequence, there may be little if any overall improvement in the nation's health.

Public health officials often point to the introduction of low-tar cigarettes in the 1960s and 1970s to illustrate the challenges of regulating reduced-risk products. The companies were careful not to make any explicit health claims when they started to market "light" and "ultralight" cigarettes, but the implicit message was that these products provided a less harmful way of smoking and many smokers believed and continue to believe that they are safer than regular-strength cigarettes. Light cigarettes emit lower levels of tar and nicotine than regular-strength cigarettes, as measured by a standardized smoking machine test developed by the Federal Trade Commission and commonly referred to as the FTC method. However, the National Cancer Institute (NCI) concluded that there is "no convincing evidence" that the introduction of such low-yield products "resulted in an important decrease in the disease burden" among smokers.[93] Many smokers who switched to low-yield cigarettes changed the way they smoked so as to maintain the desired intake of nicotine. They smoked more intensely by inhaling more deeply and more often and by covering the ventilation holes at the base of the filter. This compensatory smoking behavior exposed them to higher amounts of tobacco toxins.[94]

H.R. 1108/S. 625 would prohibit manufacturers from marketing "modified risk tobacco products" without FDA prior approval. The legislation defines modified risk tobacco products as any product:

- whose labeling or advertising indicates, explicitly or implicitly, that the product is less risky than other tobacco products or reduces exposure to a substance in the product or its smoke;
- whose manufacturer has taken any action (other than through labeling or advertising) that "would be reasonably expected to result in consumers believing" that the product or its smoke reduces risk or exposure; or
- whose labeling or advertising uses descriptors such as "light," "mild," or "low" to characterize the level of a substance in the product.

In order to gain approval to market a modified risk tobacco product, a manufacturer would have two options. The first is to submit a reduced-risk claim.

---

[93] National Institutes of Health, National Cancer Institute, Risks Associated with Smoking Cigarettes with Low Machine-Measured Yields of Tar and Nicotine, Smoking and Tobacco Control Monograph 13 (NIH Pub. No. 02-5074) (October 2001).

That would require the company to demonstrate to FDA that the product, "as actually used by consumers," will reduce the risk of tobacco-related disease to individual users and "benefit the health of the population as a whole." Alternatively, the manufacturer could assert that the product reduces exposure to a particular substance. H.R. 1108/S. 625 sets out detailed criteria for approving such a reduced-exposure claim. Those criteria, based on recommendations of the Institute of Medicine,[95] include determining that the exposure reduction is "substantial;" the substance to which exposure is reduced is harmful; the reduced exposure is anticipated to lead to a "measurable and substantial reduction" in harm among individual users; and approval of such a product is "expected to benefit the health of the population as a whole." Applications for products that make exposure-reduction claims would be approved for five years at a time. All manufacturers of approved modified risk tobacco products, whether on the basis of a reduced-risk claim or a reduced-exposure claim, would be required to conduct postmarket surveillance and report their findings on an annual basis.

If enacted into law, the modified risk provisions in H.R. 1108/S. 625 would produce immediate changes in cigarette marketing. Manufacturers would be required to stop using terms such as "light" and "low-tar" on their low-yield brands. Those brands would be permitted to remain on the market provided the manufacturers made any other changes necessary to ensure that the products did not fall under the definition of a modified risk tobacco product. For example, manufacturers have for years reported tar and nicotine yields (as measured by the FTC method) on cigarette advertising and on some very low-tar cigarette packs. Because this information implies that the product reduces risk or exposure, it too would have to be removed. Under a separate provision in the legislation, FDA would be required to develop new regulations for the testing, reporting, and public disclosure of tobacco productingredients and smoke constituents, including tar and nicotine levels (see Table 2). Those regulations would replace the current FTC method.[96]

---

[94] For a detailed discussion of the scientific and regulatory issues surrounding reduced risk tobacco products, see the Institute of Medicine's 2001 report, Clearing the Smoke: Assessing the Science Base for Tobacco Harm Reduction, Washington, DC: National Academy Press.

[95] Id.

[96] Over the past several decades, cigarette design changes have led to substantial reductions in tar and nicotine yields as measured by the FTC method. However, these machine-measured yields do not provide a reliable measure of the amount of tar and nicotine a smoker inhales. Smokers alter their smoking behavior (e.g., increasing puff volume and frequency, covering the ventilation holes with fingers or lips) to obtain sufficient nicotine to satisfy their addiction. For more information, see National Cancer Institute, Risks Associated with Smoking Cigarettes with Low Machine-Measured Yields of Tar and Nicotine (October 2001).

It is difficult to imagine a company gaining FDA approval to market a modified risk tobacco product based on a reduced-risk claim, as least in the near term. Demonstrating that the product, as actually used by consumers, will reduce risk both to the individual user and to the population as a whole requires long-term epidemiological studies. However, gaining approval for a new product on the basis of a reduced-exposure claim does not require that the manufacturer meet such stringent requirements. For example, the company would have to show that the reduced exposure is "anticipated" to lead to a reduction in harm and that the product is "expected" to benefit the health of the population as a whole. Approving modified risk tobacco products under such criteria makes postmarket surveillance all the more important as a means of monitoring the product's actual impact on public health.

H.R. 1108/S. 625 would also give FDA the authority to require the manufacturer of an approved modified risk tobacco product to comply with certain labeling and advertising requirements. Such authority could be used to place tight restrictions on the ability of manufacturers to market their modified risk products to individual tobacco users. Philip Morris and the other companies believe that they should be able to provide adult consumers with information about reduced-risk and reduced-exposure products, provided the information is accurate and not misleading, to help them make an informed choice.

Preemption of State and Local Regulation Regarding Labeling, Advertising, and Promotion

Another key issue in the debate surrounding FDA tobacco legislation involves federal preemption of state law. The Federal Cigarette Labeling and Advertising Act (FCLAA),[97] which mandates health warnings on cigarette packaging and advertising, includes the following preemption provision:

(a) Additional Statements. No statement relating to smoking and health, other than the statement required by [the labeling provisions] of this Act, shall be required on any cigarette package.
(b) STATE regulations. No requirement or prohibition based on smoking and health shall be imposed under State law with respect to the advertising or

[97] 15 U.S.C. §§ 1331-41, 4402.

promotion of any cigarettes the packages of which are labeled in conformity with the provisions of this Act.[98]

The FCLAA's introductory declaration of policy indicates that Congress did not want "commerce and the national economy ... impeded by diverse, nonuniform, and confusing cigarette labeling and advertising regulations...."[99] To that end, the act's preemption provision (1) prohibits additional health-related statements on the labels of cigarette packages that are properly labeled in accordance with the act, and (2) prevents states and localities from imposing any other "requirement or prohibition based on smoking and health" regarding the advertising and promotion of cigarettes.

The U.S. Supreme Court has issued two decisions regarding the FCLAA preemption provision. In both cases, the Court explored the constitutional questions that are raised when state statutes or common law causes of action impose requirements that conflict with federal laws that may preempt such state action (see box below).

In Cipollone v. Liggett Group Lnc, the U.S. Supreme Court held that certain types of tort actions that are brought against cigarette manufacturers under state common law are preempted by the FCLAA.[100] In the case, the son of a woman who died of lung cancer caused by smoking cigarettes sued cigarette manufacturers for causing his mother's death. His claims were based on New Jersey common (i.e., court-made) law. The plaintiff claimed, among other things, that the defendants had failed to provide adequate warnings of the health consequences of smoking cigarettes, had made and breached express warranties that their cigarettes did not present any significant health consequences, had fraudulently — through their advertising — attempted to neutralize the federally mandated warning labels, had fraudulently concealed medical and scientific data indicating that cigarettes were hazardous to health, and had conspired to deprive the public of such medical and scientific data. The defendant cigarette manufacturers argued that the FCLAA preempted state law claims. In other

[98] 15 U.S.C. § 1334. The FCLAA requires the following four rotating Surgeon General's health warnings on all cigarette packages and advertising: (1) Smoking Causes Lung Cancer, Heart Disease, Emphysema, and May Complicate Pregnancy; (2) Quitting Smoking Now Greatly Reduces Serious Risks to Your Health; (3) Smoking by Pregnant Women May Result in Fetal Injury, Premature Birth, and Low Birth Weight; and (4) Cigarette Smoke Contains Carbon Monoxide. Id. at § 1333.

[99] Id. at § 1331.

[100] 505 U.S. 504 (1992). This summary of Cipollone was written by Henry Cohen, Legislative Attorney. Supreme Court Allows Cigarette Manufacturers to Be Sued, CRS Supreme Court Review: 1991-92 Term, at 19-20.

words, the defendants argued that, having complied with the federal warning requirements, they could not be held liable for the plaintiffs mother's death, even if everything the plaintiff asserted was true.

The FCLAA contains two preemption provisions. It prohibits states from (1) requiring any statement, other than the warnings prescribed by the act, to appear on any cigarette packages, and (2) imposing any requirement or prohibition based on smoking and health with respect to the advertising or promotion of cigarettes that are labeled in conformity with the federal statute. The Supreme Court treated the two preemption provisions separately. It construed the first, prohibiting the states from requiring additional statements on cigarette packages, to supersede "only positive enactments by legislatures or administrative agencies that mandate particular warninglabels."[101] In other words, the first provision did not preempt state courts from awarding damages and thereby in effect requiring additional warning labels. However, the Court construed the second provision, prohibiting states from imposing any requirement or prohibition with respect to cigarette advertising or promotion, as broader, and as intended to preempt some common law claims.

The Court then delineated which state law claims are preempted and which may be brought. Failure-to-warn claims are preempted to the extent that they would require additional, or more clearly stated, warnings in cigarette advertising or promotions, but are not preempted to the extent that they rely on the defendants' "testing or research practices or other actions unrelated to advertising or promotion."[102] Breach of express warranty claims are not preempted because express warranties, whether set forth in advertisements or elsewhere, are not imposed by the state but arise from the manufacturer's voluntary statements. Fraudulent misrepresentation claims are preempted to the extent they are predicated on advertising statements that tended to neutralize the federally mandated warning labels, because the federal statute prohibits states from imposing prohibitions, not just requirements, with respect to cigarette advertising or promotion. However, fraudulent misrepresentations claims, and conspiracy claims, based on concealment of the hazards of smoking are not preempted insofar as they rely on a state law duty to disclose such facts through channels of communication other than advertising or promotion.

[101] 505 U.S. at 519.

[102] Cipollone v. Liggett Group Inc., 505 U.S. 504, 520, 524-25, 530-31 (1992).

Federal Preemption of State Law

The preemption doctrine derives from the Supremacy Clause of the U.S. Constitution, which establishes that the laws of the United States "shall be the supreme law of the land; and the judges in every state shall be bound thereby, any thing in the Constitution or laws of any State to the contrary notwithstanding."[a] In applying this constitutional mandate, courts have recognized both express and implied forms of preemption, which are "compelled whether Congress' command is explicitly stated in the statute's language, or implicitly contained in its structure and purpose."[b] Both types of preemption may apply to state legislation, regulations, and common law. As the Supreme Court held in Gacle v. National Solid Wastes Management Association, "the question whether a certain state action is pre-empted by a federal law is one of congressional intent. The purpose of Congress is the ultimate touchstone. To discern Congress' intent we examine the explicit statutory language and the structure and purpose of the statute."[c]

In the express preemption context, a federal statute will be deemed to supplant existing state law to the extent that it contains an explicit provision to that effect, the scope of which is determined by interpreting the language of the provision and analyzing the legislative history as necessary.[d] Where express preemption provisions are not present, federal law may preempt state law implicitly. There are several different ways to conceptualize the doctrine of implied preemption, but it is often subdivided into three general categories for purposes of analysis: (1) federal occupation of the entire field of regulation; (2) actual conflict between federal and state requirements; and (3) state requirements that frustrate congressional purpose.[e]

These standards, however, are highly speculative in their application. Indeed, the U.S. Supreme Court itself has noted that "none of these expressions provide an infallible constitutional test or an exclusive constitutional yardstick. In the final analysis, there can be no crystal clear distinctly marked formula. "[f] Thus, cases involving federal preemption of state law often hinge on the particular factual circumstances of a given case.

a. U.S. Const, art. VI, cl. 2.

b. Gacle v. National Solid Wastes Management Association, 505 U.S. 88, 97 (1992) (quoting Jones v. Rath Packing Co., 430 U.S. 519, 525 (1977)).

c. Id. at 96 (internal quotation marks and case citations omitted).

d. Jones v. Rath, 430 U.S. at 525

e. Sprietsma v. Mercury Marine, 537U.S. 51,64 (2002); see also Hines v. Davidowitz, 312 U.S. 52, 61, 77 (1941) (regarding field and frustration of purpose preemption); Florida

Lime and Avocado Growers, Inc. v. Paul, 373 U.S. 132, 142-143 (1963) (regarding conflict preemption).

f. Hines v. Davidowitz, 312 U.S. at 67.

The Supreme Court also addressed FCLAA preemption in Lorillard Tobacco Co. v. Reilly.[103] In addition to finding Massachusetts' regulations on smokeless tobacco and cigar advertising unconstitutional (discussed earlier), the Court in Lorillard ruled that the state's restrictions on cigarette advertising were preempted by the FCLAA. Specifically, the Court concluded that the regulations did relate to the "advertising or promotion" of cigarettes. It further concluded that the regulations, targeted at youth exposure to cigarette advertising, were "based on smoking and health" within the meaning of the FCLAA because "concern about youth exposure to cigarette advertising is intertwined with the concern about ... smoking andhealth."[104] The fact that the regulations governed location rather than content of advertising did not remove them from the preemption language, which covers "all 'requirements' and 'prohibitions' imposed under state law."[105] The Lorillard decision clarified that while the FCLAA preempts the ability of states to regulate the advertising and promotion of cigarettes, states retain the authority to regulate other aspects of tobacco use and sales. The FCLAA, for example, does not preempt state laws that prohibit sales to minors or restrict smoking in public places.[106]

The public health community strongly supports the elimination of the FCLAA preemption language so that states could impose their own restrictions on tobacco labeling and advertising. The tobacco companies, on the other hand, oppose any such change, in part to preserve the uniform national standards currently in effect. However, the industry also is anxious to preserve the FCLAA's preemption provision in light of the U.S. Supreme Court's ruling in Cipollone. If Congress were to amend that provision, such legislation, depending on the language, could either increase or restrict the types of lawsuits that currently may be brought against cigarette manufacturers on the basis of the warning contained on cigarette packages.

---

[103] 533 U.S. 525 (2001).

[104] Id. at 548.

[105] Id. (emphasis omitted).

[106] The FCLAA preemption provisions apply only to cigarettes and do not cover state regulation of smokeless tobacco and cigars. As discussed in an earlier section of the report, Massachusetts' outdoor advertising and point-of-sale restrictions on smokeless tobacco and cigars were found to be in violation of the First Amendment.

H.R. 1108/S. 625 appears to attempt to accommodate both sides by preserving the current language in the FCLAA preemption provision, while adding at the end the following:

> (C) EXCEPTION. Notwithstanding subsection (b), a state or locality may enact statutes and promulgate regulations, based on smoking and health ... imposing specific bans or restrictions on the time and place, and manner, but not content, of the advertising or promotion of any cigarettes.

Thus, states would continue to be prohibited from adding their own warning labels to cigarette packages, but would be permitted to regulate certain aspects of cigarette advertising and promotion, subj ect to any First Amendment challenge. For the tobacco companies, the language in subsection (b) underlying Cipollone would remain intact.[107] In addition to amending the FCLAA preemption provision, H.R. 1108/S. 625 includes a general preemption provision in the new FFDCA language that would place certain restrictions on states while allowing them to regulate the sale, advertising, and promotion of tobacco products (see Table 2).

Preemption of State and Local Regulation Regarding the Age of Sale of Tobacco Products

If H.R. 1108/S. 625 were enacted into law, the provision to be codified at FFDCA § 906(d)(3)(A)(ii) states that the Secretary of Health and Human

Services may not "establish a minimum age of sale of tobacco products to any person older than 18 years of age," via a regulation requiring restrictions on the sale and distribution of a tobacco product.[108] This provision gives rise to a dynamic that this report will refer to as a "maximum-minimum age" of 18: age 18 is the highest age that the Secretary could require an individual to attain in order to be of a minimum age to purchase tobacco products.[109] When § 906(d)(3)(A)(ii)

---

[107] See Letter from Steven C. Parrish, Senior Vice President, Corporate Affairs, Altria Group, Inc., to Senators Edward M. Kennedy and John Cornyn (February 15, 2007), [http://www.altria.com/download/pdf/ SCP_FDA_Endorsement_Senate.pdf].

[108] A regulation setting the highest minimum age of purchase at 18 years of age could be promulgated by the HHS Secretary if "the Secretary determines that such regulation would be appropriate for the protection of public health." H.R. 1108, § 101 (to be codified at § 906(d)(1)).

[109] The Secretary would have the authority, under the bill, to establish a purchase age of younger than 18. However, given the current federal law pertaining to cigarette sales to individuals under 18, it is unlikely that the Secretary would issue such a regulation. The Public Health Service Act authorizes the Secretary to "make an allotment each fiscal year for each state" to be used forApril 7,2008, "activities to prevent and treat substance abuse." 42 U.S.C. § 300x-21. Undera 1992 amendment to this statute, sponsored by Representative Michael Synar and known as the

is read in conjunction with the provision of H.R. 1108 to be codified at FFDCA § 916 (FFDCA § 917 in S. 625), it does not appear that § 906(d)(3)(A)(ii) would expressly or implicitly preempt state laws that set a higher minimum age, such as 19 years of age, to purchase tobacco products.[110] The provisions of the FFDCA to be codified at § 916 or § 917 provide that none of the rules promulgated "shall be construed to limit the authority of... a State ... to ... enforce any law ... with respect to tobacco products that is ... more stringent than, requirements established" by H.R. 1108/S. 625 "that relat[e] to orprohibit[] the sale,... access to,... or use of tobacco products by individuals of any age...." These provisions appear to serve as a limitation on the preemptive effect of § 906(d)(3)(A)(ii). However, the manner in which courts may interpret the limitation on the maximum-minimum age dynamic and apply preemption standards in general is uncertain.

Retailer Liability

The following are the potentially applicable provisions in the FFDCA under which tobacco retailers could be held liable for violations of the act. S. 625 defines a retailer as "any person who sells tobacco products to individuals for personal consumption, or who operates a facility where self-service displays oftobacco products are permitted."[111] Most liability provisions are found in the "Penalties" section of the FFDCA, § 303. H.R. 1108/S. 625 would add the phrase "tobacco product" to several sections of FFDCA § 301, which lists the prohibited acts to which the penalties in § 303 may apply. The addition of the phrase "tobacco product" would thus make the penalties section of the FFDCA, § 303,

Synar Amendment, the Secretary may make such grants "only if the State has in effect a law providing that it is unlawful for any manufacturer, retailer, or distributor of tobacco products to sell or distribute such product to any individual under the age of 18." Id. at § 300x-26(a)(l). The Synar Amendment was enacted as § 1926 of the Alcohol, Drug Abuse, and Mental Health Administration Reorganization Act, P.L. 102-321 (1992). Under the Synar Amendment, states must enforce their bans through annual random, unannounced inspections. 42 U.S.C. § 300x-26(b)(2)(A). If a state fails to comply with the federal enforcement provisions and reporting requirements on its enforcement activities, the federal government may reduce that state's federal funding for substance abuse treatment. Id. at § 300x-26(c). According to the HHS regulations, the goal of the Synar Amendment's random inspections requirement is to achieve 80% or higher compliance with laws prohibiting tobacco sales and the distribution of tobacco products to individuals under 18. 45 C.F.R. § 96-130(g).

[110] H.R. 1108, § 101 (to be codified at § 917(a)(1)). See Alaska Stat. §§ 11.76.100, 11.76.105 (2007). However, individuals under the age of 19 who are prisoners in an adult correctional facility may possess tobacco products. Alaska Stat. § 11.76.105(a).

[111] S. 625, § 101 (to be codified at § 900(13) of the FFDCA). H.R. 1108 includes the terms "government, or entity" in its definition of "retailer." H.R. 1108, § 101 (to be codified at § 900(13) of the FFDCA). The FFDCA defines "person" to include "individual, partnership, corporation, and association." FFDCA § 201(e).

applicable if a tobacco product was adulterated, misbranded, counterfeit, or if the tobacco product fell under other circumstances to be listed in § 301 of the FFDCA; for example, if a retailer sold tobacco products in violation of a no-tobacco-sale order issued under what H.R. 1108/S. 625 would establish as the new § 303(f).[112] Another prohibited act that H.R. 1108/S. 625 would establish may also apply to retailers: "The doing of any act that causes a tobacco product to be a counterfeit tobacco product, or the sale or dispensing, or the holding for sale or dispensing, of a counterfeit tobacco product."[113]

S. 625/H.R. 1108 specify when tobacco products would be adulterated or misbranded. Certain misbranding provisions would apply to retailers. For example, a tobacco product must be deemed to be misbranded "if, in the case of any tobacco product distributed or offered for sale in any State ... (B) it is sold or distributed in violation of the regulations prescribed under section 906(d)." Section 906(d) allows the HHS Secretary to promulgate regulations requiring "restrictions on the sale and distribution of a tobacco product, including restrictions on the access to, and the advertising and promotion of, the tobacco product, if the Secretary determines that such regulation would be appropriate for public health."[114] A tobacco product would also be deemed to be misbranded if it did not bear the labeling in tobacco product standards that the HHS Secretary may prescribe.[115] More generally, as it would be amended under S. 625, and potentially applicable to retailers, FFDCA § 301 prohibits the introduction, delivery for introduction, or "the receipt in interstate commerce of any ... [tobacco product] that is adulterated or misbranded, and the delivery or proffered delivery thereof for pay or otherwise."

First, if a retailer violates certain parts of FFDCA § 301, which prohibit, among other things, adulteration, misbranding, and counterfeiting of food, drugs, devices, and cosmetics (and tobacco under S. 625/H.R. 1108), the retailer may be criminally liable under penalties section, § 303(a), of the FFDCA. The maximum criminal penalty for individuals (as adjusted by 18 U.S.C. §§ 3559 and 3571) is $100,000 if the misdemeanor does not result in death, $250,000 if the misdemeanor results in death; and/or imprisonment of one year. The maximum criminal penalty for organizations (as adjusted by 18 U.S.C. §§ 3559 and 3571) is $200,000 if the offensedoes not result in death, $500,000 if the offense results in death; and/or imprisonment of one year.

---

112 S. 625, § 103 (to be codified at FFDCA § 301(jj)).
113 S. 625, § 103 (to be codified at FFDCA § 301(ll)(3)); H.R. 1108, § 103 (to be codified at FFDCA § 301(qq)(3)).
114 S. 625, § 101 (to be codified at FFDCA § 903(7)).
115 S. 625, § 101 (to be codified at FFDCA § 903(9)).

However, a retailer could escape liability for certain violations of § 301 under the good faith exceptions in § 303(c)(1), (4), and (5), if the retailer provides the name and address of the person from whom he purchased or received the article, and copies of the documents related to delivery. As specified in § 303(c)(2) and (3), retailers and others could also avoid liability for certain violations of § 301 if they receive guarantees that would transfer liability to the manufacturer or the person from whom they received or purchased the product.

Second, if a retailer violates § 301 (adulteration, misbranding, counterfeiting, etc.) after the retailer is convicted under the penalties provision § 303 for a separate violation of § 301, he is criminally liable under penalties provision § 303(a)(2). The maximum criminal penalty for individuals (as adjusted by 18 U.S.C. §§3559 and 3571) is imprisonment for not more than three years or a fine of not more than $250,000, or both. The maximum criminal penalty for organizations (as adjusted by 18 U.S.C. §§3559 and 3571) is imprisonment for not more than three years or a fine of not more than $500,000, or both.

Third, if a retailer violates § 301 with the intent to defraud or mislead, the retailer is criminally liable and faces the same potential penalties as in the second situation.

Fourth, if a retailer violates a requirement of the FFDCA which relates to tobacco products, the retailer "shall be liable to the United States for a civil penalty in an amount not to exceed $15,000 for each such violation, and not to exceed $1,000,000 for all such violations adjudicated in a single proceeding."[116] These civil penalties could be assessed in addition to the criminal penalties outlined above. There would be a hearing to assess the civil penalty under FFDCA § 303(f), and the retailer could also be subject to a no-tobacco-sale order if "the Secretary finds that a person has committed repeated violations of restrictions promulgated under section 906(d) ["restrictions on the sale and distribution of a tobacco product including restrictions on the access to, and the advertising and promotion of, the tobacco product, if the Secretary determines that such regulation would be appropriate for public health"] at a particular retail outlet."[117]

S. 625 mandates that the FTHS Secretary issue guidance defining a "repeated violation" as at least four violations in a 36-month period.[118] The guidance would also have to provide "that good faith reliance on the presentation of a false government issued photographic identification that contains a date of birth [would] not constitute a violation of any minimum age requirement for the sale of

[116] S. 625, § 103(e) (to be codified at FFDCA § 303(f)(1)(A)).
[117] S. 625, § 103(e) (to be codified at FFDCA § 303(f)).
[118] S. 625, § 103(l).

tobacco products if the retailer has taken effective steps to prevent such violations," such as "adopting and enforcing a written policy against sales to minors."[119] Furthermore, the guidance required by the bill would set civil penalties for each violation of the § 906(d) restrictions on the sale and distribution of a tobacco product, that would differ depending on whether a retailer had in place a training program that would comply with standards to be developed by the FDA.[120]

S. 625 would amend the Federal Cigarette Labeling and Advertising Act to make it unlawful for any person to sell, offer to sell, or import for sale or distribution cigarettes without the proper warning labels.[121] However, the law would not apply to retailers if the "packaging that is supplied to the retailer by a tobacco product manufacturer, importer, or distributor and is not altered by the retailer in a way that is material" to the labeling requirements.[122] Similarly, S. 625 would amend the advertising requirements of the FCLAA to make it unlawful for a retailer "to advertise or cause to be advertised within the United States any cigarette unless its advertising bears" a label specified by the FCLAA.[123] The advertising and marketing laws would only apply to retailers, "if that retailer is responsible for or directs the label statements required."[124] However, retailers would not be relieved of liability "if the retailer displays, in a location open to the public, an advertisement that is not labeled in accordance with" the advertising requirements.[125] S. 625 also specifies that the HHS Secretary must issue "regulations to require that retail establishments for which the predominant business is the sale of tobacco products comply with any advertising restrictions applicable to retail establishments accessible to individuals under the age of 18."[126]

FDA's 1996 Tobacco Rule

H.R. 1108/S. 625 would require FDA to reissue the youth access and marketing — but not the labeling — provisions from its 1996 regulation as a final rule. The final rule would become effective one year after enactment of the legislation. Anti-tobacco groups have criticized this provision, preferring language

[119] S. 625, § 103(*l*)(1)(F).
[120] S. 625, § 103(*l*)(2)(B).
[121] S. 625, § 201 (FCLAA § 4(a)(1)).
[122] S. 625, § 201 (FCLAA § 4(a)(4)).
[123] S. 625, § 201 (FCLAA § 4(b)(1)).
[124] S. 625, § 201 (FCLAA § 4(c)(4)).
[125] S. 625, § 201 (FCLAA § 4(c)(4)).
[126] S. 625, § 101 (to be codified at FFDCA § 913).

in other bills that would reinstate the 1996 tobacco rule without delay. Tobacco companies, noting that the advertising and marketing provisions of the rule have not been subj ected to constitutional review by the courts, may consider a First Amendment challenge.

Health Warnings

H.R. 1108/S. 625 would replace the existing Surgeon General's health warnings on cigarette and smokeless tobacco packaging and advertising with several new and more explicit messages (see Table 2). FDA would be given the authority to revise those warnings, add new ones, and alter their format, including, but not limited to, changing their size, location, and color. The legislation would result in an immediate change in the design and appearance of tobacco product packaging. Cigarette packaging, for example, would carry health warnings that covered at least 30% of the front and back of the pack. As previously noted, states would not be permitted to add additional health warnings.

Menthol

H.R. 1108/S. 625 would ban the use of all artificial and natural flavors in cigarettes, except menthol. Mentholated cigarettes are an important component of the U. S. cigarette industry, accounting for more than one-quarter of the approximately $70 billion domestic market. The exemption for menthol is widely viewed as an important compromise that was negotiated with Philip Morris in order to secure the company's support for the legislation. In June 2008, seven former HHS Secretaries from Democratic and Republican administrations wrote to members of the House and Senate urging them to ban the use of menthol in cigarettes. Their concern mirrors that of many in the public health community who question why menthol — by far the most widely used flavoring in cigarettes — is receiving special treatment.

The menthol exemption is controversial because mentholated cigarettes are the most popular choice among African-American smokers. According to the Surgeon General, more than three-quarters of African American smokers smoke menthol cigarettes, as compared to about one-quarter of white smokers. Public health officials hypothesize that the widespread use of mentholated cigarettes among African Americans may, in part, be the reason why they suffer from higher smoking-related health risks. Despite smoking fewer cigarettes per day and beginning smoking later in life, the years of potential life lost before the age of 65 is two times higher in black smokers than white smokers. Furthermore, African-

American teen smokers have a greater risk of developing long-term consequences from smoking than other ethnic groups, and are in danger of experiencing the negative effects of tobacco earlier in their lifetimes. Researchers point to studies suggesting that menthol smokers may be exposed to higher levels of dangerous compounds than smokers of regular cigarettes. Some menthol brands, including top-selling Newport, contain among the highest levels of nicotine among leading cigarettes. There is also evidence that it is harder to quit smoking menthol products. Tobacco companies, while acknowledging the health risks of smoking, contend that menthol does nothing to worsen those risks.

Sponsors of H.R. 1108/S. 625 argue that under FDA's broad new authority to promulgate tobacco product standards to reduce or eliminate harmful constituents, or otherwise modify the composition of tobacco products, the agency could ban menthol if it determined that such action was appropriate to protect the public health. Such a determination would have to be based on a consideration of the risks and benefits to the population as a whole, including users and nonusers of tobacco products. Meeting that standard would in all likelihood require more definitive scientific evidence than is currently available.

Table 1. Summary of McCain Tobacco Bill (105th Congress)

Topic	S. 1415 (McCain)[a]
Amendment of Federal Food, Drug, and Cosmetic Act (FFDCA)	Creates new FFDCA Chapter IX for regulating tobacco products. Defines adulterated and misbranded tobacco products. For each brand, requires manufacturers to submit annually a list of the amounts of all added ingredients and a description of the content, yield, and form of nicotine. Requires notification of modified products or release of new products. Requires annual registration of all manufacturers and biennial inspection of facilities. Authorizes regulation of the sale, distribution, advertising, promotion, and use of tobacco products in order to protect public health. Provides for good manufacturing practice regulation, subject to a tobacco product advisory committee's recommendations. Authorizes adoption (and revocation) of performance standards to reduce/eliminate nicotine or otherwise modify the composition of the product in order to protect public health: mandates notice and comment rulemaking, including consideration of impact of performance standard on consumption and development of a black market. Requires a one-year delay before new standards take effect. Requires two-year congressional review of any proposal to eliminate nicotine or ban tobacco products. Authorizes the recall of products that contain out-of-the-ordinary defects that pose serious health risks. Provides for the establishment of industry reporting requirements. Requires premarket approval of new products. Provides for judicial review of regulatory actions to issue or revoke performance standards. Provides for postmarket surveillance. Defines reduced risk product and permits marketing of suchproducts. Permits state and local authorities to adopt more stringent public health controls. [Section 101]
Marketing and advertising restrictions	Prohibits outdoor tobacco product advertising; prohibits use of human or cartoon images in advertising; prohibits Internet advertising unless site is inaccessible to minors; prohibits paying for placement of tobacco products in movies, TV, or video games; prohibits paying to glamorize tobacco use in media that appeal to minors; prohibits promotional non-tobacco merchandise bearing brand names; prohibits brand-name sponsorship of sporting and cultural events; prohibits use of recent non-tobacco trade or brand names for tobacco products. Limits size and placement of point-of-sale advertising. Requires black-on-white format for point-of-sale advertising in facilities that are accessible to minors and for advertising in publications with a significant youth readership.[b] Limits advertising in audio format to words with no music. Limits advertising in video format to static black-on-white text. [Sections 1403-1405]

Table 1. Summary of McCain Tobacco Bill (105th Congress) (Continued)

Topic	S. 1415 (McCain)[a]
Warnings, labeling, and packaging	Amends existing federal labeling laws to require new, explicit health warning labels inbold type.[c] Authorizes DHHS to revise warning labels in order to promote a greater public awareness of the risks of tobacco use. Exempts tobacco-product exports from the new labeling requirements. Mandates regulations for the testing, reporting, and public disclosure of ingredients and tobacco smoke constituents to protect the public health. [Sections 301-305, 311, 1106]
Youth access restrictions	Prohibits sales to minors; requires photo ID if under age 27; requires face-to-face transactions; bans vending machines; restricts self-service displays to adult-only facilities; allows mail-order sales subject to FDA review. [Sections 231, 1162]
Retailer licensing and registration	Requires states to license tobacco retailers. Establishes penalties for noncompliance, including license suspension and revocation. [Sections 231]
State enforcement of youth access laws	Requires states to enforce (using federal drug abuse block grant funds) laws prohibiting the sale or distribution of tobacco products to minors, and to conduct monthly unannounced inspections. States must achieve 80% compliance by year four and 90% by year seven or risk losing federal block grant funds. Repeals Synar Amendment."[d] [Sections 231-233]
Underage tobacco-use targets	Mandates an annual survey to determine the percentage of individuals under age 18 who used a tobacco product in the past 30 days, and the percentage who used each brand in the past 30 days. Sets reduction targets for underage use of cigarettes (by 40% in five years and 67% in 10 years) and smokeless tobacco products (by 25% in five years and 45% in 10 years). [Sections 201-204]
Industry penalties	Mandates industry-wide and manufacturer-specific penalties (not tax-deductible) if reduction targets for underage use are not met. Industrywide penalties capped at $2 billion a year; manufacturer-specific penalties capped at $5 billion a year. [Sections 205-206]

Table 1. Summary of McCain Tobacco Bill (105th Congress) (Continued)

Topic	S. 1415 (McCain)[a]
Smoking restrictions in public facilities	Restricts smoking in public facilities (i.e., those entered by 10 or more individuals at least one day a week), including federally owned or leased buildings, to enclosed, separately ventilated, designated smoking areas. Specifies that employees may not be required to enter smoking areas. Exempts restaurants (other than fast food), bars, private clubs, hotel guest rooms, casinos, bingo parlors, tobacco outlets, and prisons. States may opt out if they have a similar or more stringent law of their own. Allows state and local governments to enact stricter laws. [Sections 501-507]
Industry payments to National Tobacco Trust Fund	Establishes National Tobacco Trust Fund. Mandates tax-deductible industry payments into Trust Fund. Annual payments subject to inflation adjustment beginning in the sixth year, and subject to a volume-of-sales adjustment beginning in 2002. Total net revenue over first 25 years = $516 billion (estimated by Congressional Budget Office). [Sections 401-406]
State reimbursement and allocation of trust funds	Allocates 40% of the amount in the Trust Fund to reimburse states for smoking-related medical costs, 22% for tobacco-control programs, 22% for biomedical research, and 16% to provide financial assistance to tobacco farmers. [Sections 451-455]
Consent decree	Requires manufacturers, states, and the federal government to enter into voluntary, but legally binding consent decrees to enforce many of the provisions of the act (e.g., FDA regulatory authority, document disclosure, advertising and point-of-sale restrictions, annual payments). Excludes from annual liability cap (see below) any company that violates the provisions of the act. [Sections 1402-1405]
Attorneys' fees	Establishes a three-person arbitration panel to determine and award plaintiff attorneys' fees and expenses. Awards to be paid by participating manufacturers. Limits fees to $4,000/hr. [Section 1413]
Legal immunity	Allows states to settle their lawsuits in return for funding from the Trust Fund, or opt to continue with their lawsuits and forgo payments from the Trust Fund. Settles smokers' class-action lawsuits and prohibits addiction claims. Caps total annual liability at $8 billion. Modifies rule of evidence to establish an evidentiary presumption that nicotine is addictive and certain diseases are caused by tobacco use. [Sections 14061412]

Table 1. Summary of McCain Tobacco Bill (105th Congress) (Continued)

Topic	S. 1415 (McCain)[a]
Industry documents	Establishes a public tobacco document depository. Requires manufacturers to submit to FDA all documents specified in the act. Requires manufacturers to make a separate submission (with accompanying detailed log) to a three-judge panel of all documents for which they assert attorney-client privilege or trade secrecy. Requires panel to settle disputes over making such privileged documents public. [Sections 901-909, 1403]
Tobacco farmers	Incorporates two competing titles: (1) Establishes a $28.5 billion fund to provide financial assistance to tobacco farmers and their communities, maintains burley tobacco price support program, replaces flue-cured quotas with nontransferable permits. [Title X] (2) Terminates the federal tobacco price support program, establishes an $ 18 billion fund to buy out quota owners and compensate tenants. [Title XV]
Native Americans	Provides that the requirements of this act relating to the manufacture, distribution, and sale of tobacco products apply on tribal lands. Exempts tribal religious and traditional tobacco uses from the requirements of the act. Requires licensing of tribal tobacco retailers. [Sections 601-603]
Preemption of state and local actions	Allows state and local governments to adopt and enforce any additional tobacco-product control measures. [Section 5]
International tobacco control	Provides funding for international tobacco-control efforts ($350 million/yr). Prohibits use of federal funds to promote U.S. tobacco exports or to seek removal of nondiscriminatory restrictions on tobacco by foreign countries. [Sections 1101-1107]
Smuggling	Requires all manufacturers, importers, exporters and wholesalers of tobacco products to be licensed. Mandates serial numbers and export labels on packages. Requires manufacturers and distributors to submit a report for all tobacco-product export shipments. Strengthens and amends Contraband Cigarette Trafficking Act to include all tobacco products. [Sections 1131-1140]
Veterans	Provides $600 million/yr for five years from the Trust Fund for tobacco-related veterans' health care. [Section 1301]

a. Modified committee substitute bill, as amended during debate on the Senate floor: May 18 — June 17, 1998.

b. Significant youth readership is defined as having at least 2 million readers under age 18, or that readers under age 18 constitute more than 15% of the total readership.

c. (i) Federal Cigarette Labeling and Advertising Act (15 U.S.C. 1331), (ii) Comprehensive Smokeless Tobacco Health Education Act (15 U.S.C. 4401).

d. The Synar Amendment to the Public Health Service Act (42 U.S.C. 300x-26; 45 C.F.R. 96.130) requires states to enforce their laws prohibiting the sale of tobacco products to individuals under age 18. States must conduct random, unannounced inspections of retail outlets to ensure compliance with the law. States risk losing federal substance abuse block grant funds for failure to comply.

Table 2. Family Smoking Prevention and Tobacco Control Act Summary of S. 625 (as reported) and Key Differences in H.R. 1108 (as reported)

FDA Tobacco Regulatory Authority (Federal Food, Drug, and Cosmetic Act, Chapter IX)	
FDA authority over tobacco products	Creates a new FFDCA Chapter IX for regulating tobacco products, excluding any such product intended for the diagnosis, treatment, or prevention of disease, or a product for which a health claim has been made (unless the product is a modified risk product — discussed below). Does not give the Secretary regulatory authority over: (1) tobacco leaf, unless in the possession of a manufacturer; or (2) tobacco growers and warehouses. Requires the Secretary, within 90 days of enactment, to establish a Center for Tobacco Products at FDA to implement Chapter IX. Requires the Secretary to establish within FDA an office to assist small tobacco manufacturers in complying with the FFDCA. [FFDCA Sec. 901]
	H.R. 1108 includes the additional requirements that each rulemaking under this Chapter shall be in accordance with 5 U.S.C. Chapter 5, and that prior to rulemaking the Secretary shall endeavor to consult with other appropriate federal agencies. Also, unlike S. 625, the House version includes a definition of small tobacco product manufacturers (companies employing fewer than 350 employees).
Adulterated tobacco products	Specifies the conditions under which tobacco products are deemed adulterated, including: (1) contaminationby any poisonous or deleterious substance; (2) preparation, packaging, or storage under unsanitary conditions; (3) failure of a manufacturer to pay user fees (see below); (4) failure to conform to good manufacturing practice requirements (see below); or (5) the product is in violation of the requirements for modified risk products (see below). [FFDCA Sec. 902]

Table 2. Continued

FDA Tobacco Regulatory Authority (Federal Food, Drug, and Cosmetic Act, Chapter IX)	
Misbranded tobacco products	Specifies the conditions under which tobacco products are deemed misbranded, including: (1) product labeling and advertising that is false or misleading in any particular; (2) failure to include in the package labeling the name and place of business of the manufacturer and a statement of the percentage of domestic and foreign-grown tobacco in the product; (3) distribution and sale in violation of tobacco product regulations issued pursuant to the act; and (4) failure of the products' manufacturer to register with FDA, as required under the act. Authorizes the Secretary to require, by regulation, the prior approval of statements made on tobacco product labels. Prohibits the Secretary from requiring the prior approval of the content of tobacco product advertising, except for modified risk products (see below). [FFDCA Sec. 903]
Submission of data and research documents	Requires each tobacco product manufacturer or importer to submit: (1) within 6 months of enactment, a list of the amounts of all added ingredients, by brand; (2) a description of the content, yield, and form of nicotine in each product; (3) a list of the amounts of all potentially harmful smoke constituents, by brand; and (4) beginning 6 months after enactment, all documents developed after the date of enactment of this act relating to the health impact of current or future products. Requires information about a new product to be submitted at least 90 days prior to its release, and requires prompt disclosure of information about a new (or changes in the quantity of an existing) additive. At the request of the Secretary, requires each manufacturer or importer to submit any or all research documents. Within three years and annually thereafter, requires the Secretary to publish (in a format understandable to a lay person) and publicly display a list of the amounts of potentially harmful constituents, by brand. Requires the Secretary to conduct periodic consumer research to ensure the list is not misleading to the public and, after five years, to report the results of such research to Congress with recommendations for modifying or discontinuing the list. [FFDCA Sec. 904]
	H.R. 1108 specifies that the submission of the amounts of all potentially harmful constituents, by brand, (see #3 above) must begin three years after enactment.

Table 2. Continued

FDA Tobacco Regulatory Authority (Federal Food, Drug, and Cosmetic Act, Chapter IX)	
Annual registration	Requires annual registration of all tobacco product manufacturers (and others engaged in the preparation, compounding, and processing of tobacco products) and provides for public access to registration information. Requires manufacturers at the time of registration to provide a detailed product list, including copies of consumer information and product labeling. Requires registrants to file a biannual report of any changes in their product list. Mandates biennial inspection of all registered establishments. Requires foreign manufacturers and other establishments seeking to import tobacco products into the United States to register.
	Requires a manufacturer at least 90 days prior to introducing a product that was not commercially marketed as of February 15, 2007, to provide to the Secretary (in a manner prescribed by regulation) its determination that such product is substantially equivalent (within the meaning of Sec. 910, below) to another tobacco product that was in interstate commerce as of that date, and that such product is in compliance with the requirements of this act. Manufacturers that introduced a product after February 15,2007, and prior to the date that is 21 months following enactment have until that date (i.e., 21 months after enactment) to submit their report documenting substantial equivalence to a product commercially marketed as of February 15, 2007. Permits the Secretary, pursuant to regulations issues within 15 months, to exempt from these requirements certain tobacco products that have only minor differences from preexisting products. [FFDCA Sec. 905]
General regulatory controls on tobacco products	Authorizes the Secretary, by regulation, to restrict the sale, distribution, advertising and promotion of tobacco products, and access to such products, if the Secretary determines that such regulation is appropriate to protect the public health. Requires that such a determination be based on a consideration of the risks and benefits to the population as a whole, including users and nonusers of tobacco products. Requires that notices of proposed rulemaking and other published notices pursuant to authorities created under this act be made accessible to the public, and that interested person be given at least 60 days to comment.

Table 2. Continued

FDA Tobacco Regulatory Authority (Federal Food, Drug, and Cosmetic Act, Chapter IX)	
General regulatory controls (cont'd)	Prohibits limiting the sale and distribution of tobacco products to the written or oral authorization of a medical practitioner. Prohibits restricting the sale of tobacco products in face-to-face transactions in specific types of retail outlets and prohibits establishing a minimum age of sale to persons older than 18 years of age. Authorizes the Secretary, by regulation, to establish good manufacturing practice (GMP) requirements, including testing raw tobacco for pesticide chemical residues, subject to the recommendations of the Tobacco Products Scientific Advisory Committee (see below). Provides the authority to grant temporary or permanent exemptions or variances to the GMPs in response to petitions. Protects trade secrets obtained by FDA from Freedom of Information Act requests. [FFDCA Sec. 906]
	H.R. 1108 requires (as opposed to authorizes) the Secretary to issue GMP regulations, which may provide for the testing of raw tobacco for pesticide residues. It also specifies that small manufacturers (as defined in the bill) are not required to comply with such regulations until four years after they take effect. H.R. 1108 also requires the Secretary, within 18 months, to issue regulations regarding the sale and distribution of tobacco products other than by a retailer in a face-to-face exchange(e.g., Internet and mail-order sales), in order to prevent underage access to such products. It further requires the Secretary, within two years, to issue regulations regarding the promotion and marketing of tobacco products that are sold or distributed other than by a retailer in a face-to-face exchange, in order to protect minors.

Table 2. Continued

FDA Tobacco Regulatory Authority (Federal Food, Drug, and Cosmetic Act, Chapter IX)	
Tobacco product standards	Subject to subsequent revision by rulemaking, prohibits cigarettes from containing: (1) an artificial or natural flavor, other than tobacco or menthol; or (2) an herb or spice. Authorizes the Secretary to promulgate tobacco product standards to reduce nicotine, reduce or eliminate other harmful constituents, or otherwise modify the composition and testing of tobacco products, if it determines that such regulation is appropriate to protect the public health. Requires that such a determination be based on a consideration of the risks and benefits to the population as a whole, including users and nonusers of tobacco products. Requires the involvement of other federal agencies and informed persons in setting product standards, and periodic evaluation of such standards. Mandates notice and comment rulemaking, with a comment period of at least 60 days, and requires a one-year delay before new standards take effect unless the Secretary determines an earlier effective date is necessary to protect public health. In any proposed standard that determines a tobacco product constituent to be harmful, a party challenging such a determination must prove that the proposal will not reduce or eliminate health risk. Reserves for Congress the authority to ban tobacco products or reduce nicotine yields to zero. Provides for the amendment and revocation of existing standards. Permits the Secretary to refer a proposal to establish amend, or revoke a product standard to the Tobacco Products Scientific Advisory Committee (see below). The Secretary may make such a referral based on his own initiative, or upon the request of an interested person who demonstrates good cause. Within 60 days of the referral, the Advisory Committee is required to report with recommendations. [FFDCA Sec. 907]
	H.R. 1108 prohibits tobacco products containing foreign-grown tobacco with pesticide levels that exceed U.S. standards or that was grown using unapproved pesticides. It also requires the Secretary to consider the following types of information submitted in connection with a proposed tobacco product standard: (1) the technical feasibility of compliance with the standard; and (2) the impact of the standard on the creation of a black market for products that do not meet the requirements of this Chapter. Instead ofreserving for Congress the authority to ban tobacco products or eliminate nicotine, H.R. 1108 prohibits the Secretary from taking such action.

Table 2. Continued

FDA Tobacco Regulatory Authority (Federal Food, Drug, and Cosmetic Act, Chapter IX)	
Notification and recall	In the event that the Secretary determines that a tobacco product presents an unreasonable risk of substantial harm to the public health and that notification is necessary to eliminate such risk, the Secretary is authorized to issue an order to ensure adequate notification of all appropriate persons. Compliance with such an order does not relieve persons from liability under other federal or state law. Authorizes the Secretary to order the appropriate persons to cease distribution and, subject to an informal hearing, to recall a tobacco product that contains an out-of-the-ordinary defect that poses serious health risks. [FFDCA Sec. 908]
Records and reports	Requires tobacco product manufacturers and importers to establish and maintain such records and provide such information as FDA may by regulation reasonably require to assure that products are not adulterated or misbranded and to otherwise protect public health. For example, FDA may require a report from a manufacturer that becomes aware of information that reasonably suggests that one of its products may have caused or contributed to a serious unexpected adverse experience associated with the use of that product. Requires tobacco product manufacturers and importers to report any product removal from the market or other corrective action taken to reduce a health risk or remedy a violation of this Chapter. [FFDCA Sec. 909]
Premarket review	Requires premarket review of any new tobacco product (including a product in test markets) that is found not to be substantially equivalent to a product on the market as of February 15, 2007. Premarket review is not required if the new product has only minor modifications from a preexisting product (which exempts it from requiring a substantial equivalence determination). Defines substantial equivalence and specifies the types of information to be included in an application for premarket review. Requires the Secretary, on his own initiative or upon the request of an applicant, to refer the application to the Tobacco Products Scientific Advisory Committee (see below). Establishes procedures for denying an application for premarket approval, and for withdrawing or temporarily suspending such approval. Specifies that a denial shall be based on a finding that permitting the marketing of the new tobacco product is inconsistent with the protection of public health, taking into consideration the risks and benefits to the population as a whole, including users and nonusers. Investigational tobacco products may, under conditions prescribed in regulation, be exempted from the provisions of this Chapter. [FFDCA Sec. 910]

Table 2. Continued

FDA Tobacco Regulatory Authority (Federal Food, Drug, and Cosmetic Act, Chapter IX)	
Modified risk tobacco products	Requires manufacturers to obtain FDA approval in order to market modified risk tobacco products. Defines a modified risk tobacco product as: (1) a product whose labeling/advertising includes descriptors such as "light," "mild," or "low", or that claims explicitly or implicitly that the product reduces the risk of tobacco-related disease or reduces exposure to a substance; or (2) a product for which the manufacturer has taken any other action directed at consumers such that they would be reasonably expected to believe that the product reduces risk or exposure. Authorizes FDA to approve a modified risk product claim if the manufacturer demonstrates that the product, as it is actually used by consumers, will significantly reduce harm to individual tobacco users and benefit the health of the population as a whole, including users and nonusers of tobacco products. Requires FDA to make modified risk product applications available for public comment and to refer them to the Tobacco Products Scientific Advisory Committee (see below) for review. In the case of a product for which the modified risk application is limited to an explicit or implicit reduced-exposure claim, authorizes FDA to approve such a product for a five-year period (renewable) if the manufacturer demonstrates that: (1) the reduction in exposure to a harmful substance or substances is substantial; (2) the available scientific evidence shows a reasonable likelihood of a substantial reduction in risk among users; and (3) the proposed labeling and market of the product will not mislead consumers into believing that it has been demonstrated to be less harmful.

Table 2. Continued

FDA Tobacco Regulatory Authority (Federal Food, Drug, and Cosmetic Act, Chapter IX)	
Modified risk products (cont'd)	Establishes other conditions for approval of modified risk products, including the requirement that the advertising and labeling of such products enable the public to comprehend the product's risk in the context of all tobacco-related health risks. Permits FDA to require that manufacturers of approved modified risk products comply with other advertising and promotion requirements. Requires manufacturers of approved modified risk products to conduct postmarket surveillance. Permits FDA to withdraw approval, after an opportunity for an informal hearing, if it is determined that the modified risk claim is no longer valid. Requires FDA, within two years and in consultation with the Institute of Medicine and other experts, to issue regulations or guidance on the scientific evidence required for assessing modified risk tobacco products. Prohibits distributors from taking any action on a tobacco product that would reasonably be expected to result in consumers believing that the product is rendered less harmful or that it reduces or eliminates exposure to certain substances. Products for treating tobacco dependence, including cessation products, are not modified risk products if they have been approved as drugs/devices under FFDCA Chapter V. [FFDCA Sec. 911]
Judicial review	Establishes procedures for judicial review of: (1) a regulation establishing, amending, or revoking a tobacco product standard; or (2) a denial of an application for premarket approval. Pursuant to 5 U.S.C. 706(2)(A), specifies that the reviewing court will hold unlawful any agency action, findings, or conclusions found to be arbitrary, capricious, an abuse of discretion, or otherwise not in accordance with law. [FFDCA Sec. 912]
Equal treatment of retail outlets	Requires FDA to issue regulations requiring retail outlets whose predominant business is selling tobacco products to comply with any advertising restrictions applicable to retail outlets accessible to individuals under age 18. [FFDCA Sec. 913]
Federal Trade Commission jurisdiction	Nothing in this act (except where expressly provided) limits or diminishes the existing authority of the FTC to regulate the advertising, sale, or distribution of tobacco products. Requires the Secretary and the FTC Chairman to coordinate their tobacco regulatory activities. [FFDCA Sec. 914]

Table 2. Continued

FDA Tobacco Regulatory Authority (Federal Food, Drug, and Cosmetic Act, Chapter IX)	
Congressional review	Provides for congressional review of any rule promulgated under this Chapter, pursuant to 5 U.S.C. 801 et seq. [FFDCA Sec. 915]
	H.R. 1108 does not include this provision.
Ingredient and smoke constituent testing	Requires the Secretary, within two years, to issue new regulations mandating the testing and reporting of tobacco product ingredients and smoke constituents, by brand and sub-brand, that the Secretary determines should be tested to protect the public health. Such regulations may require the disclosure of testing results through for example, labels and advertisements. [FFDCA Sec. 916; FFDCA Sec. 915 in H.R. 1108]
	H.R. 1108 requires the Secretary to issue new regulations within three years ofenactment. The bill includes additional provisions relating specifically to small manufacturers (as defined in the bill) that provide additional time for compliance with the testing and reporting regulations, including extensions for limited testing laboratory capacity.
Preemption of state and local laws	Generally preserves state and local authority to regulate and tax tobacco products, but preempts all state and local requirements that relate to the following provisions in this Chapter: tobacco product standards; premarket approval; adulteration; misbranding; labeling; registration; GMPs; and modified risk products. Does not preempt state and local requirements relating to the sale, use, access to, advertising, and promotion of tobacco products. [FFDCA Sec. 917; FFDCA Sec. 916 in H.R. 1108]
Tobacco Products Scientific Advisory Committee	Within one year, requires the Secretary to establish an 12-member Tobacco Products Scientific Advisory Committee. Specifies the Committee's membership, duties, and compensation. [FFDCA Sec. 918; FFDCA Sec. 917 in H.R. 1108]

Table 2. Continued

FDA Tobacco Regulatory Authority (Federal Food, Drug, and Cosmetic Act, Chapter IX)	
Nicotine replacement products	Instructs the Secretary to: (1) at the request of the applicant, designate nicotine replacement products as fast track products under FFDCA Section 506; (2) consider approving the extended use of nicotine replacement products; and (3) consider the evidence for additional indications for nicotine replacement products, such as for craving relief or relapse prevention. Within three years, requires the Secretary to submit to Congress a report on how best to regulate, promote, and encourage the development of innovative products and treatments for tobacco dependence. [FFDCA Sec. 919; FFDCA Sec. 918 in H.R. 1108]
User fees	Establishes within the Treasury a Tobacco Product User Fee Fund. Instructs the Secretary to assess user fees (payable quarterly) on tobacco manufacturers and importers, to be deposited in the Fund, to pay for the cost of FDA tobacco regulation under this Chapter. Sets the amount of the assessment at $85 million in FY2008, $235 million in FY2009, and $450 million in FY2010, adjusted in each subsequent fiscal year to reflect the greater of: (1) the percentage change in the Consumer Price Index; (2) the percentage change in base pay for federal workers in Washington DC; or (3) the average annual change in the cost, per FTE, of FDA personnel compensation and benefits. Requires an annual upward adjustment in the total amount of fees assessed, with these additional funds to be deposited in the general fund of the Treasury, to defray any net loss in general revenue due to changes in revenue and spending resulting from enactment of this act.
	H.R. 1108 does not establish a fund within the Treasury and sets the amount of the assessment at $90.1 million in FY2008, increasing to $ 754.7 million in FY2018 and in each subsequentfiscal year (with no adjustments). Ofthe fees collected, it specifies a slightly lower amount available to the Secretary for tobacco regulation: $85 million in FY2008, increasing to $712 million in FY2018 and in each subsequent fiscal year.

Table 2. Continued

FDA Tobacco Regulatory Authority (Federal Food, Drug, and Cosmetic Act, Chapter IX)	
	Specifies that each class of tobacco products be assessed a percentage of the total assessment, based on the applicable percentages in subsection 625(c) of the Fair and Equitable Tobacco Reform Act of 2004 (P.L. 108-357). Specifies that the percentage share of fees paid by each manufacturer or importer of a particular class of tobacco products be based on that manufacturer's or importer's share of the domestic market, as determined by the Secretary of Agriculture pursuant to subsections 625(e)-(h) of P.L. 108-357. [FFDCA Sec. 920; FFDCA Sec. 919 in H.R. 1108]
	H.R. 1108, in addition, requires GAO, within three years, to report to Congress on underage tobacco use and the feasibility and impact of calculating user fees based in whole or in part on a manufacturer's youth market share.
Illicit tobacco trade	Beginning one year after enactment, requires that the tobacco product labels, packaging, and shipping containers for products intended for domestic consumption must bear the statement: "Sale only allowed in the United States." Requires the Secretary to issue regulations regarding the establishment and maintenance of records by any person who manufactures, processes, transports, distributes, packages, holds, exports, or imports tobacco products. Prohibits the Secretary from requiring retailers to maintain records of individual customer purchases. Grants the Secretary access to all records if there is reason to believe that a tobacco product is part of an illicit trade or smuggling or is a counterfeit product. Requires tobacco product manufacturers and distributors with knowledge of illegal transactions to promptly notify the Attorney General. Requires the GAO to study and, within 18 months, report on cross-border trade of tobacco products (including illicit trade) and tobacco advertising that is broadcast, transmitted, or distributed from the United States to another country. [FFDCA Sec. 921; FFDCA Sec. 920 in H.R. 1108]
	H.R. 1108 requires the GAO study to include data on the health effects of: (1) smuggled and counterfeit tobacco products; and (2) differing tax rates applicable to tobacco products. It also defines cross-border trade as international and interstate trade, including trade with Indian tribes.

Table 2. Continued

	FDA Final Tobacco Rule (August 28,1996)
	Requires the Secretary within 30 days to publish the 1996 FDA tobacco rule (minus the labeling provisions in Subpart C, and with modified definitions of "cigarettes" and other terms, pursuant to the definitions used in this act) as a final rule. The rule shall become effective no later than one year after enactment of this act.
	H.R. 1108 requires the Secretary to publish the final rule no sooner than 180 days after enactment. The bill also amends subsection 897.16(d) of the rule (prohibition on free samples of tobacco products) to permit free samples in a qualified adult-only facility (as defined).
	Tobacco Product Labeling and Advertising
Cigarette Health Warning Labels	Amends the federal cigarette labeling and advertising law[a] to require new, rotating, explicit health warning labels in bold type on cigarette packages.[b] Specifies the placement and typography of the labels. Exempts cigarette exports from the package labeling requirements. Retailers that are supplied with cigarettes in violation of these labeling requirements are not liable. Further amends the existing cigarette labeling law to require the same health warnings in cigarette advertising, and specifies the placement and typography of such warnings (as well as other required statements relating to tar, nicotine, and other constituents) in press and poster ads. Authorizes the Secretary, through rulemaking, to make adjustments to the format and type size of the act's cigarette labeling requirements or to the text, format, and type size of other required statements relating to tar, nicotine, and other constituents. Retailers are liable if they publicly display an advertisement that is not labeled in accordance with this act. Specifies that the new labeling requirements will take effect one year after enactment. Instructs the Secretary, within two years, and through rulemaking, to require color graphics depicting the negative health consequences of smoking to accompany the label requirements. Thereafter, the Secretary may, by rulemaking, adjust the text, format, and type size of any of the label requirements in order to promote a greater public understanding of the risks of tobacco use. Permits states to regulate the time, place, and manner, but not the content, of cigarette advertising and promotion.

Table 2. Continued

Tobacco Product Labeling and Advertising	
	Unlike S. 625, which requires the warning labels to occupy the top 50% of the front and rear panels of a cigarette package, H.R. 1108 requires the labels to occupy at least the top 30% of both panels. H.R. 1108 also has slightly modified requirements for the Secretary, through rulemaking, to change the required statements, require color graphics, and adjust the text, format, and type size of any other disclosures required under the FFDCA, in order to promote greater public understanding of the risks of tobacco use.
Smokeless Tobacco Health Warning Labels	Amends the federal smokeless tobacco labeling and advertising law[c] to require new, rotating, explicit health warning labels in bold type on smokeless tobacco packages.[d] Specifies the placement and typography of the labels. Exempts smokeless tobacco exports from the package labeling requirements. Retailers that are supplied with smokeless tobacco products in violation of these labeling requirements are not liable, provided they do not sell or distribute such products. Further amends the existing smokeless tobacco labeling law to require the same health warnings in smokeless tobacco advertising, and specifies the placement and typography of such warnings (as well as other required statements relating to tar, nicotine, and other constituents) in press and poster ads. Prohibits smokeless tobacco advertising on radio or television. Specifies that the new labeling requirements will take effect one year after enactment. Authorizes the Secretary, by rulemaking, to adjust the text, format, and type size of any of the label requirements, require color graphics, increase the required label area from 30% to 50% of a package's front and rear panels, and adjust the text, format, and type size of any other disclosures required under the FFDCA, in order to promote a greater public understanding of the risks of smokeless tobacco use.
	H.R. 1108 states that retailers that are supplied with smokeless tobacco products in violation of these labeling requirements are not liable. It also specifies that retailers are liable if they publicly display an advertisement that is not labeled in accordance with this Act. Finally, H.R. 1108 includes an addition provision that authorizes the Secretary, through rulemaking, to make adjustments to the format and type size of the Act's smokeless tobacco labeling requirements or to the text, format, and type size of other required statements relating to tar, nicotine, and other constituents.

Table 2. Continued

Tobacco Product Labeling and Advertising	
Tar, Nicotine, and Other Smoke Constituent Disclosure	Amends the federal cigarette labeling and advertising law[a] to require the Secretary, by rulemaking, to determine whether cigarette and other tobacco product packaging and advertising must disclose tar and nicotine yields. Requires the Secretary, by a memorandum of understanding, to resolve with the Federal Trade Commission (FTC) any differences between the tar and nicotine disclosure requirements established by the Secretary and those established by FTC under existing law. Additionally, the Secretary, by rulemaking, may require disclosure of the level of other tobacco product constituents (including smoke constituents), if such disclosure would benefit public health or otherwise increase awareness of the health risks of tobacco use, except that no such disclosure may be required on the face of any cigarette package or advertisement. Retailers are liable if they sell or distribute tobacco products that do not bear the health warning labels required under this act.
	H.R. 1108 does not include the provision making retailers liable if they sell or distribute products without the required health warning labels.
Miscellaneous Provisions (H.R. 1108 only)	
Report on minimum purchase age	Requires the Secretary to convene an expert panel and, within five years, report to Congress on the public health implications of raising the minimum purchase age for tobacco products.
Report on industry concentration	Requires FTC to study the causes and effects of concentration in the tobacco industry and report to Congress within five years and, again, within 10 years.
Indian Tribes	Requires the Secretary to ensure that the provisions of this Act and its implementing regulations, including those that relate to retail sales of tobacco product, are enforced with respect to Indian Tribes.

a. Federal Cigarette Labeling and Advertising Act (15 U.S.C. 1331). The Federal Trade Commission (FTC) administers the cigarette labeling law; the Justice Department enforces the law.

b. The new labels read: (i) WARNING: Cigarettes are addictive; (ii) WARNING: Tobacco smoke can harm your children; (iii) WARNING: Cigarettes cause fatal lung disease: (iv) WARNING: Cigarettes cause cancer; (v) WARNING: Cigarettes cause strokes and heart disease; (vi) WARNING: Smoking during pregnancy can harm your baby; (vii) WARNING: Smoking can kill you; (viii) WARNING: Tobacco smoke causes fatal lung disease in nonsmokers; and (ix) WARNING: Quitting smoking now greatly reduces serious risks to your health.

c. Comprehensive Smokeless Tobacco Health Education Act (15 U.S.C. 4401). The FTC administers and enforces the smokeless tobacco labeling law.

d. The new labels read: (i) WARNING: This product can cause mouth cancer; (ii) WARNING: This product can cause gum disease and tooth loss; (iii) WARNING: This product is not a safe alternative to cigarettes; and (iv) WARNING: Smokeless tobacco is addictive.

In: FDA Regulation of Tobacco Products ISBN: 978-1-60692-550-8
Editor: Victoria C. Lockwood, pp. 51-65

Chapter 2

TOBACCO: SELECTED LEGAL ISSUES*

Vanessa Burrows
American Law Division

Summary

Over the past decade, the courts and the Congress have been grappling with tobacco-related issues. Among these issues are the Food and Drug Administration's (FDA) attempt to regulate certain tobacco products under the Federal Food, Drug, and Cosmetic Act (FDCA); the Master Settlement Agreement (MSA) that resulted from lawsuits brought by states attorneys general against tobacco companies; federal, private party, and foreign lawsuits against tobacco companies; limits on tobacco advertising; and restrictions on selling and distributing tobacco to minors. During the 110th Congress, legislators have introduced several bills that address some of the above issues, including H.R. 1108, S. 625, S. 1162, and S.Con.Res. 21.

The FDCA gives the FDA authority to regulate food, drugs, devices, and cosmetics. In 1996, the FDA promulgated a final rule stating that, under the FDCA, it could regulate cigarettes and smokeless tobacco. In 2000, the U.S. Supreme Court, however, found that Congress had not given the FDA regulatory power over tobacco and overturned the final rule in FDA v. Brown & Williamson Tobacco Corp.

In the 1990s, states attorneys general brought lawsuits for reimbursement of their states' tobacco-related medical expenses. The states attorneys general and the tobacco companies reached a settlement in 1997, but this settlement never garnered the congressional approval needed for implementation. In 1998,

* Excerpted from CRS Report RL33719, Updated April 30, 2007

however, 46 states, the District of Columbia, five U.S. territories, and the tobacco industry signed the MSA, worth $206 billion over 26 years.

In 1999, the Clinton Administration filed a lawsuit against major tobacco companies and industry trade groups to recoup federal tobacco-related medical costs. In August 2006, the district court held that the tobacco companies violated two Racketeer Influenced and Corrupt Organization Act (RICO) claims and, among other remedies, ordered them to remove descriptors such as light, low tar, natural, mild, and ultra light from their packaging. The case is being appealed.

Since the U.S. Supreme Court's 1992 decision in Cipollone v. Liggett Group Inc., individual and class action lawsuits have been brought against tobacco companies under theories such as fraudulent representation, conspiracy, breach of express warranty, and failure to warn. The private party suit section of this CRS report discusses the recent decision to certify as a class action the first light cigarettes case in a federal court, Schwab v. Philip Morris U.S.A., Inc., as well as other selected state class actions. Suits brought in federal courts by foreign governments for medical care costs resulting from tobacco-related illnesses have not been successful.

Tobacco advertising is restricted at the federal, state, and local levels. The Federal Cigarette Labeling and Advertising Act (FCLAA), state laws and the MSA, and local ordinances limit tobacco advertising in ways such as prohibiting radio and television advertisements, compelling the use of health warning labels, banning the use of cartoons, and requiring individuals to have contact with a sales person before purchasing tobacco products. Additionally, federal law plays a role in enforcing laws that prohibit tobacco sales to minors.

Introduction

Over the past decade, the courts and the Congress have been grappling with tobacco-related issues. Among these issues are the Food and Drug Administration's attempt to regulate tobacco under the Federal Food, Drug, and Cosmetic Act; the Master Settlement Agreement that resulted from lawsuits by states attorneys general against tobacco companies; federal, private party, and foreign lawsuits against tobacco companies; limits on tobacco advertising; and restrictions on selling and distributing tobacco to minors. During the 110th Congress, legislators have introduced several bills that address some of the above issues, including H.R. 1108, S. 625, S. 1162, and S.Con.Res. 21.

The FDA's Ability to Regulate Tobacco Products

Congress passed the Federal Food, Drug, and Cosmetic Act[1] (FDCA) in 1938 in response to a tragedy in which 100 people died after taking a drug containing a highly toxic substance. The statute increased the Food and Drug Administration's (FDA) enforcement power, gave the FDA jurisdiction over previously unregulated cosmetics and devices, and instituted safety measures such as requiring instruction labels on drugs and a pre-market approval process for new drugs.[2] The FDCA also "prohibited false therapeutic claims for drugs."[3] Since 1938, the law has been amended numerous times.[4] Under the FDCA, "drugs" fall into three categories or an inclusive fourth category comprised of articles intended to become a component of any of the other three categories. These three categories are (1) "articles recognized in the official United States Pharmacopoeia" or a similar standard-setting body for prescriptions and over-the-counter medications; (2) "articles intended for use in the diagnosis, cure, mitigation, treatment, or prevention of disease in man or other animals"; and (3) "articles (other than food) intended to affect the structure or any function of the body of man or other animals."[5] When determining whether an article is a drug under the second or third categories, the agency takes the intent of the vendor into account. However, even if a vendor does not intend to sell an item as a drug, the FDA can still govern it as a drug.[6] The term "drug" does not include food or dietary supplements.[7]

The FDCA defines "device" as:

> an instrument, apparatus, implement, machine, contrivance, implant, in vitro reagent, or other similar or related article, including any component, part, or accessory . . . which does not achieve its primary intended purposes through chemical action within or on the body of man or other animals and which is not dependent upon being metabolized for the achievement of its primary intended purposes.[8]

---

[1] 21 U.S.C. § 301 et seq.

[2] James T. O'Reilly, Food and Drug Administration, § 3.4 (2005).

[3] FDA's Role in Protecting and Promoting Public Health, available at [http://www.fda.gov/centennial/centennial_files/textonly/index.html].

[4] Amendments to the FDCA have included a broad range of topics such as food and color additives, animal drugs, drug abuse control, infant formula, saccharin labeling, orphan drugs, nutrition information and food allergen labeling, prescription drug marketing and importation, safe medical devices, and dietary supplements.

[5] 21 U.S.C. § 321(g)(1).

[6] O'Reilly, § 13.3. Sunscreen is one example of such a product. Id.

[7] 21 U.S.C. § 321(g)(1)(D).

[8] 21 U.S.C. § 321(h).

In addition, in order to be a "device" under the FDCA, an item must fall within one of three categories that are nearly identical to those the FDCA uses to define a "drug" (see above). In classifying an item as a device, the FDA takes into account the manufacturer's intent as to whether it is a device. This intent may be "indicated in the product's labeling" and by how the manufacturer promotes, distributes, and sells the product.[9]

Combinations of drugs and devices are also regulated by the FDA. A drug-device combination product is defined to include, among other things, a product that contains a drug and a device that "are physically, chemically, or otherwise combined or mixed and produced as a single entity."[10] Examples of this type of drug-device combination product include insulin inj ector pens, metered dose inhalers, transdermal patches, and catheters with antimicrobial coating.[11]

Under the theory that cigarettes and smokeless tobacco are "a combination of a drug, device, or biologic product,"[12] the FDA issued a final rule[13] in 1996 that would have given the agency jurisdiction over these tobacco products as drugs,devices, or both drugs and devices.[14] The agency's rule concentrated on cigarettes and smokeless tobacco because the FDA did not have "sufficient evidence that [cigars] are drug delivery devices" and "because young people predominantly use cigarettes and smokeless tobacco products."[15] The FDA found that nicotine was a drug under the above statutory definition providing that a drug is an article that "affect[s] the structure or any function of the body."[16] This was because nicotine "causes addiction and other significant pharmacological effects on the human body."[17] The FDA further concluded that cigarettes and smokeless tobacco have "device components that deliver nicotine to the body" and are

[9] O'Reilly, § 18.2.

[10] 21 CFR § 3.2(e)(1).

[11] FDA, Frequently Asked Questions, [http://www.fda.gov/oc/combination/faqs.html#_Toc88444656].

[12] 21 U.S.C. § 353; FDCA § 503(g).

[13] Regulations Restricting the Sale and Distribution of Cigarettes and Smokeless Tobacco to Protect Children and Adolescents, 61 FR 44396 (1996). For a detailed description of the FDA's 1996 final rule that would have restricted the sale of tobacco products, advertising, and labels, as well as the federal district and court of appeals cases leading up to the Supreme Court's decision in FDA v. Brown & Williamson Tobacco Corp., see CRS Report RL32619, FDA Regulation of Tobacco Products: A Policy and Legal Analysis, by C. Stephen Redhead and Vanessa Burrows.

[14] 61 FR 44400.

[15] 61 FR 44422 (quoting Regulations Restricting the Sale and Distribution of Cigarettes and Smokeless Tobacco Products to Protect Children and Adolescents, 60 FR 41314, 41322 (to be codified at 21 C.F.R. pts. 801, 803, 804, 897) (proposed August 11, 1995)).

[16] 21 U.S.C. § 321(g)(1).

[17] Annex to the Final Rule, Nicotine in Cigarettes and Smokeless Tobacco is a Drug and These Products are Nicotine Delivery Devices Under the Federal Food, Drug, and Cosmetic Act: Jurisdictional Determination, 61 FR 44619, 44628-29 (1996).

"intended" by tobacco manufacturers to do so.[18] In the case of cigarettes, the FDA said that the device that delivers the drug nicotine has "components [that] work together upon combustion outside the body to form a nicotine-containing aerosol, which then delivers nicotine to the body when inhaled by the smoker."[19] With smokeless tobacco, the device is a component that provides "nicotine to the consumer in a form that is palatable and absorbable by the buccal mucosa," which is the lining inside the cheeks and lips.[20]

Implementation of the final rule would have enabled the FDA to regulate cigarettes and smokeless tobacco, including their access by minors, labeling, and advertising, under the "device" portion of the FDCA.[21] In order to reach tobacco advertising and youth access to these tobacco products, the FDA rule relied on the agency's already-established authority to restrict the sale, use, and distribution of a potentially harmful device or a device that requires "collateral measures necessary for its use [if] the Secretary determines that there cannot otherwise be reasonable assurance of its safety and effectiveness."[22] Under the FDA's interpretation of the FDCA in the 1996 rule, the FDA could have issued rules on recordkeeping and manufacturing as well as reporting requirements in the event of contamination or "serious adverse events that are not well-known . . . in the scientific community."[23] With the 1996 rule in place, the FDCA also would have allowed the FDA to place cigarettes in one of three classes of devices ranging from devices that present minimal harm to users to devices requiring FDA approval because of the risk for illness and the need for regulatory control. However, before the FDA could implement its final rule or issue any further regulations, the tobacco industry challenged the final rule. The industry argued that the FDCA did not permit the FDA to regulate tobacco, that the FDA could not regulate tobacco products because such items did not claim to provide health benefits, and that the FDA's advertising restrictions violated commercial speech protections guaranteed by the First Amendment.

In FDA v. Brown & Williamson Tobacco Corp., the U.S. Supreme Court held that the FDA did not have the statutory authority under the FDCA to regulate

[18] 61 FR 44628-29; 21 U.S.C. § 321(h).
[19] 61 FR 44649-50.
[20] 61 FR 44650.
[21] Regulations Restricting the Sale and Distribution of Cigarettes and Smokeless Tobacco to Protect Children and Adolescents, 61 FR 44396, 44400 (1996). The agency asserted that in order "to provide the most effective protection to the public health," it had discretion in choosing whether to regulate combination products as drugs or devices, and it chose to regulate cigarettes and smokeless tobacco as devices. Id. at 44400.
[22] 21 U.S.C. § 360j(e); FDCA § 502(e).
[23] 61 FR 44615-18.

tobacco products as drug-delivery devices, and therefore did not reach the First Amendment issue.[24] The Court used the test it had articulated in Chevron U.S.A., Inc. v. Natural Resources Defense Council,[25] which addresses congressional intent and agency discretion:

> When a court reviews an agency's construction of the statute which it administers, it is confronted with two questions. First, always, is the question whether Congress has directly spoken to the precise question at issue. If the intent of Congress is clear, that is the end of the matter; for the court, as well as the agency, must give effect to the unambiguously expressed intent of Congress. If, however, the court determines Congress has not directly addressed the precise question at issue, the court does not simply impose its own construction on the statute ... Rather, if the statute is silent or ambiguous with respect to the specific issue, the question for the court is whether the agency's answer is based on a permissible construction of the statute.[26]

The Court found that Congress had spoken on the issue of the FDA's authority to regulate tobacco products under the FDCA by passing laws — not administered by the FDA — that dealt with marketing, labeling, and education regarding tobacco products. Specifically, the Court held that the FDA's interpretation of the FDCA, in its 1996 final rule, was contrary to Congress's intent "expressed in the FDCA's overall regulatory scheme and in tobacco-specific legislation that [Congress] has enacted."[27] According to the Court, if the FDA had regulatory authority over tobacco under the FDCA, then tobacco companies could not market their products, and tobacco products would have to be banned because they are not safe or effective.[28]

State Suits and the Master Settlement Agreement[29]

Beginning in 1994, 41 states and Puerto Rico began filing lawsuits against tobacco companies for reimbursement of tobacco-related medical expenses, particularly Medicaid expenditures. These lawsuits eventually culminated in the 1998 Master Settlement Agreement (MSA), but initially they resulted in a June

---

[24] FDA v. Brown & Williamson Tobacco Corp., 529 U.S. 120, 142-43 (2000).
[25] 467 U.S. 837 (1984).
[26] Id. at 842-43.
[27] FDA, 529 U.S. at 126.
[28] Id. at 135-37.
[29] For detailed explanations of the proposed 1997 National Tobacco Settlement and the 1998 Master Settlement Agreement, see CRS Report RL32619, FDA Regulation of Tobacco Products: A Policy and Legal Analysis, by C. Stephen Redhead and Vanessa Burrows.

1997 settlement between states attorneys general and tobacco manufacturers. The 1997 settlement incorporated all the provisions of the FDA's 1996 tobacco rule, discussed above. The 1997 proposal included changes to the FDCA and other federal statutes, and required congressional legislative action in order to take effect. The 1997 agreement, however, never took effect because Congress did not approve legislation implementing the settlement. Attempts by the 105th Congress to pass such legislation — comprised of the settlement and additional measures such as financial penalties if targets for reducing underage tobacco use were not met — ended when Senator John McCain's bill was defeated on two procedural votes on June 17, 1998, after an extended floor debate.[30] The negotiated agreement would have resulted in tobacco-related medical reimbursement payments to states of $368.5 billion for 25 years and then $15 billion per year after the first 25 years. Additionally, tobacco companies would have paid for programs to reduce adolescent tobacco use. This settlement would also have granted immunity to tobacco manufacturers from future lawsuits and ended existing class action lawsuits filed by smokers and their relatives, as well as nicotine addiction claims.

After the defeat of Senator McCain's bill, the major cigarette companies resumed contractual negotiations with the states to settle the lawsuits. In November 1998, attorneys general from 46 states, the District of Columbia, and five U.S. territories signed the MSA with the major tobacco companies. Four states — Mississippi, Florida, Texas, and Minnesota — did not join the MSA, but instead settled individually with the tobacco companies. The MSA did not settle individual, union, private health care, or class action suits. Through the MSA, states will receive annual payments of $206 billion over 26 years. Each state needed to and did obtain its trial court's approval to receive the MSA funds. The MSA also prohibited certain advertising, marketing, and promotion of tobacco products (see the Tobacco Advertising section below).

Of the $61 million paid to the states by tobacco companies to date, states have spent less than 8% on anti-smoking endeavors, according to a March 2007 article by the American Bar Association Journal.[31] Government Accountability Office figures indicate that states have spent even less on tobacco control, which it defines as effortsto include prevention, education, enforcement, and cessation

[30] National Tobacco Policy and Youth Smoking Reduction Act, S. 1415, 105th Cong. (1998). See, e.g., 144 Cong. Rec. S5494-5511 (June 1, 1998); 144 Cong. Rec. S5737-62 (June 9, 1998); 144 Cong. Rec. S6275-89 (June 12, 1998).

[31] Mark Curriden, Up in Smoke, A.B.A. Journal, March 2007, at 27.

services.[32] States have allocated 30% of their MSA payments to health care, including Medicaid, health insurance, and hospitals; 22.9% towards budget shortfalls; 7.1% to general purposes; 6% towards infrastructure; 5.5% to education; 5.4% to debt service on securitized funds; 3.5% on tobacco control; and 7.8% to other projects.[33] The states have not allocated 11.9% of their MSA payments.[34]

As noted, the MSA grew out of lawsuits by the states seeking reimbursement for their medical expenses on behalf of tobacco users. If a third party, such as a tobacco company, causes an illness or injury to someone, and a state provides medical care for that illness or injury, as, for example, out of Medicaid funds, then the state may sue the third party for reimbursement of such funds. Because the federal government pays for at least 50% of each state's Medicaid costs, by law the federal government is entitled to its share of any reimbursements of Medicaid funds that a state receives from a third party that caused an illness or injury on which Medicaid funds were expended.[35] With respect to the MSA, however, Congress enacted P.L. 106-31 (2000), which authorizes the states to keep reimbursements they receive from third parties.[36]

The Federal Lawsuit

The federal lawsuit against major tobacco companies and industry trade groups began under the Clinton Administration in 1999 as a way for the U.S. government to recover tobacco-related medical costs paid by federal health care programs. The Department of Justice (DOJ) was seeking (1) restitution for money paid by the federal government's health care programs for treatment and care of persons with tobacco-related diseases, (2) a disgorgement of the profits that the tobacco industry allegedly earned by violating the Racketeer Influenced and Corrupt Organizations Act (RICO), and (3) orders preventing fraud and future violations of the law, such as racketeering or making false, deceptive, or misleading statements about cigarettes; as well as orders that the defendants take

[32] Lisa Shames, Acting Director, Natural Resources and Environment, GAO, Testimony Before the Committee on Health, Education, labor, and Pensions, U.S. Senate (February 27, 2007), Tobacco Settlement: States' Allocations of Payments from Tobacco Companies for Fiscal Years 2000 through 2005, at 14.

[33] Shames, supra note 32. Section 10908 of the Farm Security and Rural Investment Act of 2002 mandates that GAO report on "all programs and activities that States have carried out using funds received under all phases of the Master Settlement Agreement of 1997." P.L.107-171.

[34] Shames, supra note 32.

[35] 42 U.S.C. § 1396b(d)(2)(B).

[36] FY1999 Emergency Supplemental Appropriations Act (P.L. 106-31), § 3031.

certain actions, such as issuing corrective statements, disclosing research, and funding smoking cessation programs.[37] In 2000, the U.S. District Court for the District of Columbia dismissed two claims by the government that would have provided for recovery under the Medical Care Recovery Act as well as under the Medicare Secondary Payer Act provisions of the Social Security Act.[38] The suit then proceeded under two RICO claims, 18 U.S.C. § 1962(c) and (d).[39] Section 1962(c) criminalizes the association of persons, including corporations, with enterprises that conduct their affairs through "a pattern of racketeering activity," which means that they commit two or more specified crimes within ten years. Section 1962(d) outlaws conspiracies to violate § 1962(c) or related provisions regarding racketeering activities. The government alleged that a pattern of racketeering activity existed because the defendants defrauded "individual smokers of their property (i.e., the money they spent on cigarettes)."[40]

During the trial, the defendants appealed the U.S. District Court for the District of Columbia's opinion allowing the remedy of disgorgement — the giving up of the tobacco industry's past profits gained by its deceptive practices — to the U.S. Court of Appeals for the D.C. Circuit. In 2005, the court of appeals overturned the district court's opinion, thus limiting the remedial measures that the district court could impose if it found that the defendants had violated RICO.[41] Because the court of appeals allowed only forward-looking injunctive relief, the DOJ could not recover the $280 billion disgorgement that had been sought for tobacco profits earned since 1971 for marketing to youth.[42] The court of appeals stated that injunctive relief under RICO[43] must focus on preventing future wrongdoing rather than on punishing past conduct. Noting that Congress explicitly crafted a set of remedial measures in the RICO statute and likely did not intend to provide other remedies, the court of appeals was "reluctant" to infer an additional remedy such as disgorgement.[44]

---

[37] United States v. Philip Morris Inc., No. 99-2496, 1-2, 91-92 (D.D.C. filed February 2001) (DOJ First Amended Complaint).

[38] For a detailed explanation of the government's claims under the Medical Care Recovery Act and the Medicare Secondary Payer Act, see CRS Report RS20091, The Federal Lawsuit Against Tobacco Companies to Recover Health Care Costs, by Henry Cohen. This report has been archived and is available from the author.

[39] For additional information on RICO, see CRS Report 96-950, RICO: A Brief Sketch, by Charles Doyle.

[40] United States v. Philip Morris Inc., et al., No. 99-2496, 48 (D.D.C. 2000).

[41] United States v. Philip Morris Inc., 396 F.3d 1190 (D.C. Cir. 2005), cert. denied546 U.S.960 (2005).

[42] Anthony J. Sebok, The Federal Government's RICO Suit Against Big Tobacco, Findlaw.com, October 4, 2004, available at [http://writ.lp.findlaw.com/sebok/20041004.html].

[43] 18 U.S.C. § 1964(a).

[44] Philip Morris, 396 F.3d at 1200.

In August 2006, the U.S. District Court for the District of Columbia ruled that the defendants had violated RICO. The court found that the tobacco companies and trade industry organizations had conspired "to deceive the American public about the health effects of smoking and environmental tobacco smoke, the addictiveness of nicotine, the health benefits from low tar, 'light' cigarettes, and their manipulation of the design and composition of cigarettes in order to sustain nicotine addiction."[45]

Although, as mentioned above, the U.S. Court of Appeals prevented the district court from imposing the remedy of disgorgement, the district court ordered the defendants to pay DOJ's legal costs, which totaled approximately $1.93 million.[46] The district court also enjoined the defendants from using descriptors such as low tar, light, mild, and natural on their cigarette packaging and advertisements; ordered the defendants to place "onserts" or stickers with corrective statements on their packaging and to issue statements in newspapers and on television and retail displays; and extended the length of time that tobacco companies must make documents produced in litigation available to the public, a requirement that originated in the MSA.

Both the tobacco companies and the DOJ have filed notices of appeal with the U.S. Court of Appeals for the D.C. Circuit.[47] Neither of these notices states the parties' particular objections to the lower court decision, but rather enables the parties to appeal any and all parts of the judgment. In addition, pending the outcome of their appeal, the defendants moved to stay the district court's order banning them from using descriptors such as light or low tar. On September 28, 2006, the district court denied the defendants' request for a stay, concluding that "loss of market share, if it results from imposing an appropriate remedy to prevent and restrain past violations of the law, may well be the price Defendants have to pay for violations of RICO."[48] The defendants therefore filed a motion with the U.S. Court of Appeals for the D.C. Circuit requesting an emergency stay of the district court order pending appeal.[49] On October 31, 2006, the court of appeals

---

[45] United States v. Philip Morris U.S.A., Inc., No. 99-2496, 1 (D.D.C. September 8, 2006) (amended memorandum opinion).

[46] United States v. Philip Morris U.S.A., Inc., No. 99-2496 (D.D.C. filed October 2, 2006) (bill of costs).

[47] United States v. Philip Morris U.S.A., Inc., No. 99-2496 (D.D.C. September 11, 2006) (Philip Morris U.S.A. Inc., Altria Group, Inc., British American Tobacco Ltd., R.J. Reynolds Tobacco Co., Brown & Williamson Corp., and Lorillard Tobacco Co. Notices of Appeal); United States v. Philip Morris U.S.A., Inc., No. 99-2496 (D.D.C. October 16, 2006) (DOJ Notice of Appeal).

[48] United States v. Philip Morris U.S.A., Inc., No. 99-2496, 1 (D.D.C. September 28, 2006) (memorandum opinion on stay appeal).

[49] United States v. Philip Morris U.S.A., Inc., Nos. 06-5267 - 06-5272 (D.C. Cir. October 2, 2006) (defendants' emergency motion to stay the judgment).

granted the stay, enabling the tobacco companies to continue using descriptors such as ultra light or natural until the court rules on the appeal.[50]

On March 16, 2007, the U.S. District Court for the District of Columbia responded to a motion by certain defendants for clarification of the court's August 2006 order restricting the defendant's use of marketing descriptors such as natural and ultra lite. Noting that RICO provisions have effect outside the United States if the illegal activity abroad "causes a 'substantial effect' within the United States," the court concluded that the defendants were prohibited from using such marketing descriptors and express or implied health messages internationally as well as in the United States.[51] Several countries, including Australia, Brazil, and European Union members, currently prohibit marketing descriptors such as light and low-tar.[52] The district court order banning the use of marketing descriptors domestically and internationally will not take effect immediately because of the appellate court's stay of the district court order and the pending appeal. Defendants Philip Morris U.S.A., Inc., Altria, R.J. Reynolds, Brown & Williamson, Lorillard, and BATCo. may be affected in differing degrees by the international application of the order due to the level of their international sales.

Private Party Suits

Prior to 1992, tobacco lawsuits were typically individual product liability and negligence suits brought by smokers or their relatives seeking damages for smoking-related illnesses. The tobacco industry generally prevailed in these cases by arguing that the Federal Cigarette Labeling and Advertising Act (FCLAA),[53] which required warning labels, preempted plaintiffs' claims that the tobacco companies had a duty to warn consumers.[54] In some cases, however, tobacco manufacturers prevailed by arguing that smokers assumed the risks of smoking.[55] Then, in 1992, in Cipollone v. Liggett Group, Inc., the U.S. Supreme Court made it more feasible for smokers to recover. Although the Court held that federal laws requiring warning labels[56] precluded states from imposing additional requirements

[50] Appeals Court Puts Ruling Against Big Tobacco on Hold, Wash. Post, November 1, 2006, at A9.

[51] United States v. Philip Morris U.S.A., Inc., No. 99-2496, 6, 8 (D.D.C. March 16, 2007) (memorandum opinion accompanying Order #1028).

[52] Judge Extends 'Light' Cigarette Ban Overseas, CNNMoney.com, March 16, 2007.

[53] 15 U.S.C. § 1331-41.

[54] See, e.g., Pennington v. Vistron Corp., 876 F.2d 414 (5th Cir. 1989); Forster v. R.J. Reynolds Tobacco Co., 437 N.W.2d 655, 660 (Minn. 1989).

[55] See Brief for Petitioner at 13-14, n.3, Philip Morris U.S.A., Inc. v. Williams, 549 U.S. (filed July 2006) (No. 05-1256) (and cases cited therein).

[56] 15 U.S.C. §§ 1331-41, 4402.

on cigarette advertising and labeling, and therefore precluded lawsuits alleging that the federally required warning labels were inadequate, the Court stated that federal law did not preclude "state-law damages actions." Examples of state-law damages actions include failure-to-warn lawsuits based on tobacco companies' "testing or research practices or other actions unrelated to advertising or promotion," or claims of breach of express warranty, fraudulent representation, and conspiracy.[57]

This section now examines selected recent suits brought by private parties after Cipollone. In addition to the class action and individual suits discussed below, tobacco companies have been sued by their own shareholders for decreased stock prices due to deceptive practices, and by insurance companies for medical expenses resulting from fraud, conspiracy, racketeering, misrepresentation, and antitrust violations.

Long-term Marlboro smokers filed a class action suit, Caronia v. Philip Morris U.S.A., Inc., seeking to have the manufacturer provide low dose CT scans for lung cancer on an annual basis or more frequently if the scan shows signs of cancer.[58] The plaintiffs allege that Philip Morris's "wrongful design, manufacturing, and marketing" places them at a higher risk for lung cancer.[59] Philip Morris expects the court to dismiss the case because "most states don't recognize medical monitoring as a remedy or cause of action."[60] Previous lawsuits asking for medical monitoring as relief have not been successful.[61] Additionally, the utility of CT scans for lung cancer is a subject of debate.[62]

In the federal class action lawsuit Schwab v. Philip Morris U.S.A., Inc., lead plaintiff Barbara Schwab sued six tobacco companies in the U.S. District Court for the Eastern District of New York, alleging that the tobacco industry committed fraud and misled customers by marketing light cigarettes as less dangerous than regular cigarettes.[63] On September 25, 2006, the Schwab case became the first light cigarettes, or "lights," case to receive class certification from any federal

---

[57] Cipollone v. Liggett Group Inc., 505 U.S. 504, 520, 524-25, 530-31 (1992).

[58] Caronia v. Philip Morris U.S.A., Inc., No. 06-224 (E.D.N.Y. January 19, 2006).

[59] Sean Wajert, Medical Monitoring Claim Pursued in New York State, Washington Legal Foundation Legal Opinion Letter, Vol. 16, No. 15 (June 2, 2006).

[60] Peter Geier, Smokers Sue Tobacco Company for Lung Scans, Nat'l L. J., November 21, 2006.

[61] Id.

[62] Gina Kolata, Researchers Dispute Benefits of CT Scans for Lung Cancer, N.Y. Times, March 7, 2007.

[63] Schwab v. Philip Morris U.S.A., Inc., No. 04-CV-1945 (E.D.N.Y. September 25, 2006) (memorandum and order), available at [http://www.nyed.uscourts.gov/pub/rulings/cv/2004/04cv1945mo.pdf]. The defendant tobacco companies in the Schwab case are R.J. Reynolds Tobacco Co., Brown & Williamson Tobacco Corp., British American Tobacco Ltd., Lorillard Tobacco Co., Liggett Group Inc., and Philip Morris U.S.A., Inc.

court. The class includes individuals who purchased light cigarettes since the first light cigarette was introduced in 1971. The class could be extended to include individuals who bought low-tar cigarettes.[64] The court found that the MSA does not preclude the suit because, in the MSA, the states, not individual smokers, were compensated. On October 6, 2006, the defendants asked the U.S. Court of Appeals for the Second Circuit to review the federal district court's decision to certify the class action lawsuit and sought a stay pending review.

In most states, courts reportedly have denied class action status to plaintiffs for private lawsuits against tobacco companies.[65] However, in Florida, class action status was granted by the Circuit Court of Miami-Dade County in Engle v. Liggett Group, a case against tobacco companies and industry trade groups in which a jury awarded $145 billion in punitive damages. After the jury verdict, however, the classof up to 700,000 Florida smokers was de-certified by Florida's Third District Court of Appeal.[66] On July 6, 2006, the Florida Supreme Court upheld the decision to decertify the class.[67] The court stated that causation and the proportion of the defendants' fault was too individualized to be litigated as a class action suit.[68] To maintain a class action suit, the issues that the plaintiffs have in common must predominate over the individual plaintiffs' issues. In this case, the Florida Supreme Court found, individual plaintiffs' issues predominated. Such issues included whether cigarettes, or some other factor, caused the plaintiffs illness, and the percentage of fault that should be attributed to each defendant tobacco company if a plaintiff smoked multiple brands. The court did uphold smaller individual damage awards of $2,850,000 and $4,023,000 for two Florida cancer patients.

The Florida Supreme Court decision did not prevent individual smokers (or families of deceased smokers) from filing individual lawsuits instead of a class action. The court upheld most of the jury's findings that cigarettes are addictive, defective, and unreasonably dangerous products that cause diseases.[69] This aspect of the court's decision gives plaintiffs an advantage in any individual lawsuits they may file because the individuals will not have to prove these findings again — that cigarettes are addictive, defective, and unreasonably dangerous. A jury awarded $37.5 million for medical expenses, pain and suffering, and loss of consortium to Yolanda Lukacs. She was the widow of former Engle class action

---

[64] Id. at 540.

[65] Anthony Sebok, The Federal Government's RICO Suit Against Big Tobacco, Findlaw.com, October 4, 2004, available at [http://writ.lp.findlaw.com/sebok/20041004.html].

[66] Liggett Group, Inc. v. Engle, 853 So. 2d 434 (Fla. Dist. Ct. App. 2003).

[67] Engle v. Liggett Group, Inc., 2006 Fla. LEXIS 1480; 31 Fla. L. Weekly S 464 (Fla. 2006).

[68] Engle, 2006 Fla. LEXIS 1480, at *5.

[69] Id. at *7-*8.

member John Lukacs, who sued cigarette manufacturers in an individual suit that was allowed due to his terminal condition. However, the court has not entered a final judgment in the Lukacs case or ordered a trial for punitive damages, as the defendants are awaiting a decision from the U.S. Supreme Court granting or denying certiorari in the Engle case.[70]

On December 15, 2005, the Supreme Court of Illinois overturned a verdict of $7.1 billion in compensatory damages and $3 billion in punitive damages in the consumer-fraud and deceptive trade practices class action of Price v. Philip Morris U.S.A., Inc.[71] An Illinois circuit court had certified a class that consisted of 1.14 million plaintiffs who bought Cambridge Lights and Marlboro Lights in Illinois from the time that the cigarettes were first placed on the market until February 2001. The plaintiffs in Price alleged that tobacco companies committed fraud by advertising light cigarettes as having lower tar and nicotine levels and leading consumers to think that such cigarettes were safer to smoke than full flavor cigarettes.[72] The court heldthat the Federal Trade Commission had authorized light and low-tar labeling and therefore that Philip Morris U.S.A., Inc. could not be held liable as long as the company complied with Federal Trade Commission requirements, even if the terms were false or misleading. The U.S. Supreme Court denied certiorari on November 27, 2006, thus allowing the ruling of the Illinois Supreme Court to stand.

In August 2002, the California Supreme Court enabled individuals to sue tobacco companies by holding that a statute[73] granting tobacco manufacturers immunity from products liability suits applied only from the date of the statute's enactment on January 1, 1988, until the statute's repeal effective January 1, 1998. The court found that general tort principles applied to conduct before and after the ten-year immunity period.[74] In a separate case decided on the same day, the court also found that the immunity statute did not prohibit lawsuits alleging that tobacco additives create an unreasonably dangerous product "that exposed smokers to dangers beyond those commonly known to be associated with cigarette smoking."[75] In a more recent ruling, Grisham v. Philip Morris, the California Supreme Court held that the state's two year statute of limitations for filing a physical injury claim starts to run after a "smoker is diagnosed with a disease

---

70 Forrest Norman, Lawyers for Tobacco Plaintiff Want $37.5Million Judgment OK'd, Daily Bus. Rev., March 16, 2007.

71 2005 Ill. LEXIS 2071 (Ill. 2005). The Illinois Supreme Court denied the class's motion for rehearing on May 5, 2006.

72 Melanie Warner, Big Award on Tobacco is Rejected by Court, N.Y. Times, July 7, 2006, at C1.

73 Cal. Civ. Code § 1714.45, repealed by 1997 Cal. Stat. ch. 570, § 1.

74 Myers v. Philip Morris Cos., Inc., 28 Cal. 4th 828 (Cal. 2002).

75 Naegele v. R.J. Reynolds Tobacco Co., 28 Cal. 4th 856 (Cal. 2002).

caused by the cigarettes."[76] The ruling did not address whether the statute of limitations would have run if an individual was diagnosed with more than one illness, "[f]or example, if a smoker were diagnosed with emphysema five years ago and then lung cancer last month — but only files suit after the lung cancer diagnosis — the statute of limitations may have run."[77] Defendant tobacco companies had argued that the statute of limitations should begin when smokers discover they are addicted to cigarettes.[78]

Foreign Suits in U.S. Federal Courts

The Governments of Guatemala, Nicaragua, and Ukraine sued major American tobacco companies in the U.S. District Court for the District of Columbia for money they had spent on medical care for their citizens' tobacco-related illnesses. The Government of Guatemala alleged that the tobacco companies misrepresented the dangers of cigarette smoking, and as a result, the Guatemalan government waited before making efforts to shrink its smoking population.[79] Reasoning that "the injurythat [the nations] purportedly suffered occurred only as a consequence of the harm to individual smokers," the district court dismissed the lawsuit.[80]

The U.S. Court of Appeals for the D.C. Circuit affirmed the dismissal, noting that it concurred with seven circuits "that the alleged injuries of the third-party payors are too remote to have been proximately caused by the defendants' alleged conduct."[81] The court also held that the foreign governments did not have standing "unless there is a clear indication by the Supreme Court or one of the two coordinate branches of government to grant such standing" to foreign nations to sue in the U.S. on behalf of their foreign citizens.[82] The foreign governments had argued that they were suing on behalf of their people and were "seeking to protect their governments' treasuries."[83] On October 29, 2001, the U.S. Supreme Court denied certiorari, which allowed the court of appeals decision to stand.

---

[76] Millie Lapidario, Tobacco Claims Will Start Smoking Again, Thanks to Calif. Ruling, The Recorder, February 20, 2007.

[77] Id.

[78] Id.

[79] Saundra Torry, Cigarette Firms Sued by Foreign Governments, Wash. Post, January 17, 1999, at A12.

[80] Guatemala v. Tobacco Inst., Inc., 83 F. Supp. 2d 125, 129 (D.D.C. 1999).

[81] Guatemala v. Tobacco Inst., Inc., 249 F. 3d 1068, 1069 (D.C. Cir. 2001), cert. denied, 534 U.S. 994 (2001).

[82] Id. at 1073.

[83] See id. at 1072.

Tobacco Advertising: Federal Regulations, MSA Restrictions, and Local Ordinances[84]

The Federal Cigarette Labeling and Advertising Act (FCLAA) limits advertising of tobacco products.[85] The act prevents advertising of cigarettes, little cigars, and smokeless tobacco via electronic communications under the jurisdiction of the Federal Communication Commission, such as radio and wire communications, as well as broadcast, satellite, and cable television. In combination with other federal statutes, the act requires health warning labels on cigarette and smokeless tobacco packaging, as well as on all cigarette and most smokeless tobacco advertisements.[86] The health warnings must be rotated several times per year according to a manufacturer-submitted plan approved by the Federal Trade Commission.[87] Cigars are not subjected to similar advertising and warning restrictions. Because of the FCLAA's preemption provision, states cannot impose their own health warning labels on cigarettes.[88]

The FCLAA's preemption provisions do not apply to the MSA because the states and tobacco manufacturers voluntarily agreed to waive "any and all claims thatthe provisions of this Agreement violate the state or federal constitutions."[89] The MSA restricted tobacco advertising in several ways, although it did not restrict certain forms of advertising, such as print and online advertisements or marketing inside retail locations.[90] The MSA banned cartoons; tobacco advertising on public transportation; sponsorship of certain team and league sports; stadium naming rights; gifts to minors of non-tobacco merchandise in exchange for proofs of purchase of tobacco products; free samples of tobacco products in places other than adult-only facilities; signs outside stores larger than 14 square feet; and billboards in arenas, stadiums, malls, and arcades. However,

---

[84] For information on federal advertising laws related to alcohol, tobacco, mail (including junk mail), telephone, commercial email (spam), and the Federal Trade Commission Act, see CRS Report RL32177, Federal Advertising Law: An Overview, by Henry Cohen.

[85] 15 U.S.C. § 1331-41.

[86] 15 U.S.C. §§ 1331-41, 4402. Federal law does not require warning labels on outdoor billboards that advertise smokeless tobacco. 15 U.S.C. § 4402(a)(2).

[87] 15 U.S.C. §§ 1333(c)(1), 4402(c).

[88] 15 U.S.C. § 1334(b); Cipollone v. Liggett Group Inc., 505 U.S. 504 (1992).

[89] Master Settlement Agreement, p. 99, available at [http://www.naag.org/backpages/naag/tobacco/msa/msa-pdf/1109185724_1032468605_cigmsa.pdf].

[90] Since the 1998 MSA, the tobacco industry has increased its spending on marketing in ways that comply with the MSA, such as paying "bonuses to retailers who meet sales targets and post in-store signs." Tobacco manufacturers also offer "direct-mail coupons good for a free pack for each purchase of two." Myron Levin, Tobacco Deal Yet to Clear the Air, LA Times, November 27, 2003.

the MSA allows advertisements that are located within and not visible outside of adult-only facilities.[91] Within MSA limitations, tobacco companies may still sponsor certain musical, sporting, and cultural events. The MSA also bans the sale and distribution of merchandise with tobacco product brand names, except for at brand-name sponsored events. The MSA prohibits payments to the media for the promotion, mention, or use of tobacco products, except for adult-only media. Moreover, the MSA prohibits tobacco companies from targeting or promoting tobacco to minors.[92]

Though states attorneys general signed and trial courts ratified the MSA, several states and cities created additional restrictions on tobacco advertising. For example, Baltimore passed ordinances prohibiting tobacco and alcohol advertisements on billboards, except for commercial and industrial zones of the city. The U.S. Court of Appeals for the Fourth Circuit upheld Baltimore's ordinances in two cases,[93] finding that they do not violate the First Amendment.[94]

In 1999, the Massachusetts Attorney General promulgated advertising restrictions — on cigarettes, smokeless tobacco, little cigars, and cigars — that he intended to fill the gaps left by the MSA. The regulations prohibited all sizes of outdoor tobacco advertisements within 1,000 feet ofplaygrounds, schools, and parks, including advertisements located within a store that were visible from the outside of that store. The rules also imposed a similar 1,000-foot state ban on point-of-sale retail displays if the displays were less than five feet tall and located in storesaccessible to youth.[95] Additionally, the attorney general restricted tobacco promotions, samples, and cigar labels; banned self-service displays; and required customers to have contact with a sales person before handling or purchasing tobacco products.[96] In 2001, however, the U.S. Supreme Court held in Lorillard Tobacco Co. v. Reilly that the FCLAA preempted Massachusetts' outdoor advertising and point-of-sale restrictions for cigarettes, because the FCLAA preempts state regulations of cigarette advertising and promotion.[97] Therefore, the Court struck down that portion of the regulations. The Court noted, however, that

---

[91] Master Settlement Agreement, p. 18.

[92] Id. at 14-21.

[93] Penn Advertising of Baltimore, Inc. v. Schmoke, 101 F.3d 332 (4th Cir. 1996), cert. denied, 520 U.S. 1204 (1997); Anheuser-Busch v. Schmoke, 101 F.3d 325 (4th Cir. 1996), cert. denied, 520 U.S. 1204 (1997).

[94] For further information on First Amendment issues raised by advertising laws, see CRS Report 95-815, Freedom of Speech and Press: Exceptions to the First Amendment, by Henry Cohen.

[95] Mass. Regs. Code tit. 940, §§ 21.04, 22.06.

[96] Lorillard Tobacco Co. v. Reilly, 533 U.S. 525, 534-36 (2001).

[97] Id. at 551-52.

the FCLAA preemption provisions do not apply to smokeless tobacco or cigars, or restrictions on cigarette sales.[98]

Therefore, the Court had to reach the issue of whether Massachusetts' outdoor and point-of-sale advertising regulations violated the First Amendment, which guarantees freedom of speech.[99] Though Massachusetts had a compelling interest in protecting youth from tobacco products, the Court found that the restrictions on outdoor advertising of cigars and smokeless tobacco were overbroad in that they prohibited advertising "in a substantial portion of the major metropolitan areas of Massachusetts," included oral communications, and imposed burdens on retailers with limited advertising budgets.[100] The Court also upheld challenges by smokeless tobacco and cigar companies to the outdoor advertising restrictions on the grounds that adults have a right to information and the tobacco industry has a right to communicate truthful speech on legal products.[101] The Justices then struck down the similar 1,000-foot state ban on point-of-sale retail displays for cigars and smokeless tobacco under five feet tall in stores accessible to youth. They noted that the prohibition did not advance the goal of preventing minors from using tobacco products because some children are taller than five feet and others can look up at their surroundings.[102] According to one source, at least 20 state and local laws have been repealed as a result of Lorillard.[103]

Finally, as to the question of Massachusetts's regulation of cigarette, smokeless tobacco, and cigar sales, the cigarette petitioners did not argue that the FCLAA preempted Massachusetts law.[104] As a result, the Court evaluated arguments from cigarette, smokeless tobacco, and cigar petitioners that certain sales restrictions violated the First Amendment. The Court upheld restrictions banning self-service displays and requiring customers to have contact with a sales person before handling or purchasing tobacco products.[105] According to the

[98] Id. at 553.

[99] The First Amendment applies to advertising, but the U.S. Supreme Court has held that it "affords a lesser protection to commercial speech than to other constitutionally guaranteed expression" and analyzes commercial speech differently from other forms of expression. United States v. Edge Broadcasting Co., 509 U.S. 418, 426 (1993); see Central Hudson Gas & Elec. Corp. v. Public Serv. Comm'n of N.Y., 447 U.S. 557, 566 (1980) (four-part test for commercial speech analysis).

[100] Lorillard, 533 U.S. at 562, 564-65.

[101] Id. at 564. Additionally, the Court reasoned that the attorney general's restriction on in-store advertising that can be viewed from the outside "presents problems in establishments like convenience stores, which have unique security concerns." Id. at 565.

[102] Id. at 566.

[103] David L. Hudson Jr., Tobacco Ads, Speech topic - Advertising & First Amendment, [http://www.firstamendmentcenter.org/speech/advertising/topic.aspx?topic=tobacco_alcohol].

[104] Lorillard, 533 U.S. at 566.

[105] Id. at 567.

Justices, the state had a substantial interest in preventing minors from accessing tobacco products, and the regulation was narrowly tailored so as not to significantly affect adult access to tobacco products.[106]

Restrictions on Selling and Distributing Tobacco to Minors

All 50 states ban tobacco sales to individuals under age 18, and federal law plays a role in this restriction.[107] The Public Health Service Act authorizes the Secretary of Health and Human Services (HHS) to "make an allotment each fiscal year for each state" to be used for "activities to prevent and treat substance abuse."[108] Under a 1992 amendment to this statute, sponsored by Representative Michael Synar and known as the "Synar Amendment," the Secretary may make such grants "only if the State has in effect a law providing that it is unlawful for any manufacturer, retailer, or distributor of tobacco products to sell or distribute such product to any individual under the age of 18."[109]

Under the Synar Amendment, states must enforce their bans through annual random, unannounced inspections.[110] If a state fails to comply with the federal enforcement provisions and reporting requirements on its enforcement activities, the federal government may reduce that state's federal funding for substance abuse treatment.[111] According to the HHS regulations, the goal of the Synar Amendment's random inspections requirement is to achieve 80% or higher compliance with laws prohibiting tobacco sales and the distribution of tobacco products to individuals under 18.[112]

---

[106] Id. at 569.
[107] Barnaby J. Feder, U.S. Imposes Rules on Tobacco Sales to Minors, NY Times, January 19, 1996.
[108] 42 U.S.C. § 300x-21.
[109] 42 U.S.C. § 300x-26(a)(1). The Synar Amendment was enacted as § 1926 ofthe Alcohol, Drug Abuse, and Mental Health Administration Reorganization Act, P.L. 102-321 (1992).
[110] 42 U.S.C. § 300x-26(b)(2)(A).
[111] Id. at § 300x-26(c).
[112] 45 C.F.R. § 96-130(g).

In: FDA Regulation of Tobacco Products
Editor: Victoria C. Lockwood, pp. 67-71
ISBN: 978-1-60692-550-8

Chapter 3

STATEMENT OF ANDREW C. VON ESCHENBACH, COMMISSIONER OF FOOD AND DRUGS BEFORE SUBCOMMITTEE ON HEALTH, COMMITTEE ON ENERGY AND COMMERCE, UNITED STATES HOUSE OF REPRESENTATIVES ON 'H.R. 1108, FAMILY SMOKING PREVENTION AND TOBACCO CONTROL ACT'(OCTOBER 3, 2007)

Introduction

Mr. Chairman and Members of the Subcommittee, I am Andrew C. von Eschenbach, M.D., Commissioner of Food and Drugs at the United States Food and Drug Administration (FDA or the Agency). I regret that I will not have the opportunity to appear before you at this hearing because the Committee was not able to resolve the issue of witness paneling within the allotted time for the hearing.

For the last three decades, I have been engaged in the war on cancer both professionally and personally. Throughout my professional career, I have been privileged to serve in a variety of roles with a similar purpose and commitment---to help assure the health and welfare of patients and the public. As many of you may know, I spent many years at The University of Texas MD Anderson Cancer

Center as an oncologist, researcher, and educator. In my time as a practicing oncologist, I treated numerous patients suffering the ill effects of tobacco. I came to know first hand the life-threatening conditions caused by tobacco products and the tremendous suffering that is taking a toll on patients, their families and friends, and society as a whole. I then served for four and a half years as Director of the National Cancer Institute (NCI) before coming to FDA as Commissioner. Today, I sit before you as a physician, scientist, clinician, and regulator. As a three time cancer survivor, I am involved not just professionally but am personally committed to the fight against cancer and the resulting suffering and death. I am grateful for this Subcommittee's work in minimizing the effects of tobacco use in this country.

Health Effects of Tobacco Use

Although tobacco use has declined in this country, its effects are so detrimental that it remains one of the most important -- if not the most important -- public health issue we face. The 2004 Surgeon General's Report entitled, "The Health Consequences of Smoking," noted that during the period 1995-1999, smoking caused approximately 440,000 premature deaths in the U.S. annually, leading to 13.2 years of potential life lost for male smokers, and 14.5 years lost for female smokers. The list of diseases and conditions caused by smoking has been expanded to include abdominal aortic aneurysm, acute myeloid leukemia, cervical cancer, kidney cancer, pancreatic cancer, stomach cancer, pneumonia, periodontitis, and cataract. These are in addition to diseases previously known to be caused by smoking, including bladder, esophageal, laryngeal, lung, oral, and throat cancers, chronic lung diseases, coronary heart and cardiovascular diseases, as well as reproductive effects and sudden infant death syndrome. Tobacco users face nicotine addiction, increased risk of cancer from consumption of carcinogens, increased risk of heart disease from exposure to chemicals, and lung disease resulting from inhaled irritants.

We concur with the Surgeon General's conclusions that measures to prevent smoking initiation need to be a multiplex, integrated strategy and initiatives need to be strong and enforced, especially among adolescents and young adults. FDA must continue to work with the drug and device industries to ensure that smokers have a variety of options to help them treat the problem of nicotine addiction.

Federal and State Efforts on Tobacco

FDA is privileged to be among the other Federal and state agencies that are participating in some way to reduce tobacco use. It is clear, however, that the problem remains. We must continue to be innovative in our approaches and concentrate on achieving results.

Many agencies within the Department of Health and Human Services are working to address this major public health problem. FDA has worked to help develop and approve nicotine replacement products that help smokers quit, such as nicotine gum and patches, many of which are readily available over the counter to smokers who wish to quit. FDA has approved other drug products that do not contain nicotine that help smokers quit using other modes of action, including bupropion and most recently (spring 2006) varenicline. There are a variety of other non-nicotine containing smoking cessation products in the pipeline in various stages of development.

In addition, the Centers for Disease Control and Prevention (CDC), NCI, the Agency for Healthcare Research and Quality (AHRQ), the Substance Abuse and Mental Health Services Administration (SAMHSA), and the National Institute on Drug Abuse (NIDA) are all actively involved in the fight to reduce tobacco use. These agencies conduct comprehensive tobacco control and prevention programs, which serve to educate the American public on the dangers of tobacco, especially American youth. They conduct surveillance and research and collaborate with public health organizations in the prevention of tobacco use and smoking cessation programs. Finally, the Office of the Surgeon General has been especially active in the campaign against tobacco use by following up the 2004 Report with subsequent studies on the health effects of exposure to second-hand smoke and other efforts.

The states are also engaged in a variety of methods to limit smoking. All fifty states have adopted legislation prohibiting sales of tobacco to individuals under 18. Many states also limit smoking in some public locations. Most state health departments run educational programs aimed at prevention and limiting the number of smokers.

Despite the numerous Federal and state initiatives, tobacco still claims hundreds of thousands of lives every year. This is unacceptable. We have the opportunity here to explore novel solutions to the lingering problem of tobacco.

H.R. 1108

FDA shares the goal of H.R. 1108, the "Family Smoking Prevention and Tobacco Control Act," – to reduce tobacco use in this country. We agree with the need to address this significant public health problem. But we have concerns with the bill's proposed means to achieve those objectives. The Agency has three primary categories of concern with the proposed role for FDA.

First, we have concerns that the bill could undermine the public health role of FDA. Second, we have concerns about aspects of the bill that may be extremely difficult for FDA to implement. And third, we have significant concerns about the resources that would be provided under the bill and the expectations it might create. Let me elaborate on each of those areas.

First, FDA is a public health agency, structured to facilitate and regulate the development of products that promote and protect the public health. The Agency enjoys widespread public support for its role in defining and assuring effectiveness and safety of products they consume. Our responsibility includes approving products based on scientific evidence that benefits of the product outweigh the risks. We have extensive experience in such evaluations and we have developed finely tuned methodologies.

H.R. 1108 would ask us to apply this framework to tobacco products that, when used as intended, produce disease rather than promote health. FDA cannot "approve" a tobacco product in this context, because there is no scientific context to determine benefit to outweigh the numerous risks. It will be very challenging to transform existing science into a logical regulatory structure. There is little science available to the FDA on which to base decisions on tobacco product standards (such as reducing or eliminating harmful constituents, reducing the amount of nicotine in products, or requiring changes to tobacco product components) or premarket approval.

Associating the Agency with the approval of these inherently dangerous products would undermine the Agency's mission. Indeed, associating any agency whose mission is to promote public health with the approval of inherently dangerous products would undermine its mission and likely have perverse incentive effects. This proposed legislation would direct FDA to regulate tobacco products in a variety of ways, most significantly by the establishment of tobacco product standards, pre-market approval of new tobacco products, and standards for the sale of modified risk tobacco products. Approval of tobacco products that are dangerous to health even if used as directed runs directly counter to FDA's historical mission to protect and promote the public health by reviewing and approving products that prevent and treat disease, not products whose only impact on health is to cause disease.

In addition, the provisions authorizing pre-market approval of new and reduced risk tobacco products are of special concern. Most fundamentally, we are concerned that FDA "approval" of tobacco products may become confused with the Agency's regulation of therapeutic products such as drugs and devices. For example, the bill provides potential loopholes for "grandfathered" and "substantially equivalent" products, which will be permitted to stay on the market. We are concerned that the public will believe that products "approved" by the Agency are safe and that this will actually encourage individuals to smoke more rather than less.

As another example, the bill would attempt to apply current requirements for medical products such as drugs and medical devices to tobacco products. These include adverse event reporting, adulteration and misbranding, and record keeping. These concepts are not applicable to inherently dangerous tobacco products. One example of the awkwardness of applying medical product standards to tobacco products is contained in the bill's definition of an adulterated tobacco product. Section 902 of the bill provides that a "tobacco product shall be deemed to be adulterated if—'(1) it consists in whole or in part of any filthy, putrid, or decomposed substance, or is otherwise contaminated by any added poisonous or added deleterious substance that may render the product injurious to health.'"

Tobacco products, however, are intrinsically injurious to health, i.e. adulterated according to this definition. This concept, therefore, does not fit when applied to the regulation of tobacco products. There are other examples in the bill where similar problems would arise.

The bill also appears to call for FDA to perform functions that are outside of the Agency's expertise, including, for example to investigate and prevent cigarette smuggling.

The final issue of concern that I would like to discuss today is that of resources and expectations under this bill. As I am sure you are all aware, FDA is operating in a dynamic time. We are striving to meet new challenges. Just last week, the President signed the Food and Drug Administration Amendments Act of 2007 that will allow us to continue to evolve and undertake our mission of protecting the public health. Were H.R. 1108 enacted, FDA would need to create an entirely new "tobacco center" to implement the detailed program created by the bill.

By far, the most important and daunting challenge would be to develop the expertise necessary to carry out the functions called for by this bill. FDA does not have expertise regarding customarily marketed tobacco products and, therefore, would have to establish an entirely new program and hire new experts. Creating the appropriate organizational structure and hiring experts in the field of tobacco control and related sciences and other experts needed to staff the program at every level is considerably more challenging than simply filling identified vacancies in an existing program.

The provisions in this bill would require substantial resources and FDA may not be in a position to meet all of the activities within the proposed user fee levels. The $85 million in fiscal year (FY) 2008, $175 million in FY 2009, $300 million in FY 2010 and subsequent years of user fees adjusted by an inflation factor, is not sufficient to implement the complex program created by the bill. In addition, the bill does not authorize appropriations for start-up costs that would be associated with establishing a new product center. As a consequence of this, FDA may have to divert funds from its other programs, such as addressing the safety of drugs and food, to begin implementing this program.

Finally, FDA also would need a considerable amount of time, to implement the program created by the bill. The legislation authorizes or requires the Agency to publish numerous regulations and other documents.

The bill also requires the Agency, in a short timeframe, to issue a regulation originally published in 1996 that relies on data and information that are a decade old and would need to be updated to reflect the latest science. Many of the timeframes provided, ranging from 30 days to 2 years after the bill is enacted, are unworkable especially considering the expectation that we produce these documents while we are creating an entirely new program from the ground up. These timeframes unduly and unfairly raise the public's expectations about what the Agency could accomplish in a given period of time. In the best of circumstances when scientific results point to a clear regulatory approach, rulemaking typically involves at least a three-year process. In situations where the science is less fully developed or the issues are complex or controversial, and both are the case here, regulation development requires much more time.

Conclusion

I share with you the desire to reduce tobacco use in America. FDA believes it can continue to contribute to the decline in tobacco use in keeping with its primary mission by facilitating access to smoking cessation programs and therapies that have evidence of effectiveness, and by supporting sponsors who choose to pursue the development of these products. However, FDA is open to considering other roles for the Agency, if appropriate. Let me assure you that

FDA is committed to joining you and other government and private organizations in efforts to minimize the devastating effects caused by tobacco use in a manner consistent with the Agency's mission.

INDEX

A

access, 3, 6, 10, 11, 23, 24, 25, 43, 44, 45, 46, 50, 55, 56, 61, 63, 71, 85, 92
accounting, 47
achievement, 69
acute myeloid leukemia, 88
addiction, 8, 9, 14, 33, 36, 51, 70, 73, 76, 88
additives, 69, 80
adjustment, 51, 62
administrative, 14, 39
Administrative Procedure Act, 14
adolescents, 10, 31, 88
adult, 5, 6, 21, 22, 23, 25, 29, 30, 31, 33, 34, 37, 43, 85
adulteration, 9, 44, 45, 61, 91
adults, 21, 22, 23, 27, 28, 29, 34, 84, 88
adverse event, 71, 91
advertisement, 46, 64, 65, 66
advertisements, 11, 21, 29, 30, 39, 61, 76, 82, 83
advertising, vii, 1, 3, 6, 7, 10, 11, 13, 14, 15, 16, 17, 19, 23, 25, 27, 28, 29, 31, 32, 35, 36, 37, 38, 39, 41, 42, 44, 45, 46, 47, 49, 51, 54, 55, 59, 60, 61, 63, 64, 65, 66, 67, 68, 70, 71, 73, 78, 80, 82, 83, 84
aerosol, 71
African Americans, 47
age, 7, 8, 11, 15, 27, 30, 42, 43, 45, 46, 47, 50, 52, 53, 56, 60, 66, 85
Alaska, 43
alcohol, 82, 83, 84
alternative, 34, 66
amendments, 27, 32
American Cancer Society, 23
American Heart Association, 23
American Jobs Creation Act, 26
aneurysm, 88
animals, 69
anti-smoking, 17, 34, 73
antitrust, 78
aortic aneurysm, 88
application, 32, 40, 58, 59, 60, 77
appropriations, 92
arbitration, 15, 51
assessment, 62, 63
Attorney General, 30, 63, 83
Australia, 77
authority, vii, 1, 2, 3, 4, 5, 8, 10, 11, 12, 13, 14, 15, 17, 18, 19, 20, 21, 22, 23, 24, 25, 26, 27, 28, 29, 32, 33, 34, 37, 41, 42, 43, 47, 48, 51, 53, 56, 57, 60, 61, 67, 71, 72
awareness, 50, 66

B

behavior, 35, 36

behavioral aspects, 24
benefits, 2, 19, 28, 30, 33, 34, 48, 55, 57, 58, 62, 71, 76, 90
binding, 51
bipartisan, vii, 1
birth, 45
black market, 8, 15, 22, 49, 57
bladder, 88
Boston, 31
Brazil, 77
buccal mucosa, 71
buildings, 16, 51
bupropion, 89
burn, 34
Bush administration, 20
Bush Administration, vii, 1

C

cable television, 82
cancer, 66, 78, 79, 81, 87, 88
capacity, 24, 61
caps, 7
Carbon, 38
carcinogens, 33, 88
cardiovascular disease, 88
case law, 19
cataract, 88
catheters, 70
causation, 79
CDC, 89
Centers for Disease Control, 89
certification, 78
cervical cancer, 88
channels, 39
chemicals, vii, 2, 27, 88
Chevron, 12, 72
chewing, 3, 34
children, vii, 2, 10, 11, 15, 16, 25, 27, 28, 31, 32, 66, 84
cigarette smoking, 80, 81
cigarettes, vii, 1, 2, 3, 4, 7, 8, 9, 10, 11, 13, 14, 20, 21, 22, 23, 29, 31, 32, 34, 35, 38, 39, 41, 42, 46, 47, 50, 57, 64, 66, 67, 68, 70, 71, 74, 76, 78, 79, 80, 81, 82, 83
Cincinnati, 30
citizens, 81
classes, 71
classification, 9
Clean Air Act, 12
clinician, 88
Clinton Administration, 68, 74
Co, 3, 29, 40, 41, 76, 77, 78, 80, 83, 84
collateral, 10, 71
Columbia, 17, 68, 73, 75, 76, 77, 81
combustion, 34, 71
commerce, 38, 44, 55
commercial email, 82
common law, 38, 39, 40
communication, 29, 31, 39
communities, 52
community, 19, 23, 26, 34, 41, 47, 71
compensation, 61, 62
compliance, 16, 22, 43, 50, 53, 55, 57, 61, 85
components, 9, 70, 90
composition, vii, 2, 3, 5, 25, 27, 33, 48, 49, 57, 76
compounds, 14, 24, 33, 48
concealment, 39
concentration, 66
conflict, 38, 40, 41
conformity, 38, 39
Congress, vii, 1, 2, 4, 5, 6, 11, 12, 13, 15, 16, 17, 19, 20, 24, 25, 26, 27, 28, 32, 33, 38, 40, 41, 49, 50, 51, 52, 54, 57, 62, 63, 66, 67, 68, 69, 72, 73, 74, 75
Congressional Budget Office, 51
consent, 26, 51
conspiracy, 39, 68, 78
Constitution, 40
constraints, 15
construction, 12, 72
Consumer Price Index, 62
consumers, 2, 9, 23, 27, 29, 31, 35, 36, 37, 59, 60, 77, 80
consumption, 6, 21, 24, 25, 33, 43, 49, 63, 88
contamination, 71
control, 4, 10, 16, 17, 18, 25, 52, 69, 71, 73, 89, 92
corporations, 75

cosmetics, 44, 67, 69
costs, 14, 18, 30, 51, 68, 74, 76, 92
counterfeit, 44, 63
counterfeiting, 44, 45
Court of Appeals, 11, 75, 76, 79, 81, 83
courts, 39, 40, 43, 47, 67, 68, 79, 83
covering, 35, 36
craving, 62
crimes, 75
cross-border, 63
CRS, 1, 2, 19, 28, 38, 67, 68, 70, 72, 75, 82, 83
CT, 78
CT scan, 78
customers, 78, 83, 84

D

danger, 48
death, 38, 44, 88
debt, 17, 74
debt service, 17, 74
decisions, 28, 32, 38, 90
defects, 49
defendants, 38, 39, 74, 75, 76, 77, 79, 80, 81
definition, 8, 13, 34, 36, 43, 53, 70, 91
defraud, 45
delivery, vii, 2, 3, 24, 44, 45
demand, 33
denial, 58, 60
Department of Health and Human Services, 16, 89
Department of Justice, 74
Department of Justice (DOJ), 74
desire, 92
dietary, 69
disclosure, 3, 15, 17, 21, 23, 36, 50, 51, 54, 61, 66
Discovery, 30
discretionary, 10
diseases, 34, 51, 88
disputes, 15, 52
distribution, vii, 1, 3, 6, 7, 10, 15, 24, 25, 42, 43, 44, 45, 46, 49, 50, 52, 54, 55, 56, 58, 60, 71, 83, 85
District of Columbia, 17, 68, 73, 75, 76, 77, 81
dominance, 5
download, 22, 42
draft, 26
drug abuse, 50, 69
drug delivery, 70
drugs, 8, 9, 10, 13, 18, 19, 21, 25, 44, 60, 67, 69, 70, 71, 91, 92
duties, 61

E

education, 2, 13, 18, 26, 53, 66, 74
educational programs, 89
electronic communications, 82
Emergency Supplemental Appropriations Act, 18, 74
emphysema, 81
employees, 51, 53
Energy and Commerce Committee, 2, 27
environment, 24
environmental tobacco, 76
EPA, 12
ethnic groups, 48
European Union, 77
expenditures, 14, 72
expert, 66
expertise, 91
exports, 50, 52, 63, 64, 65
exposure, 21, 23, 35, 36, 37, 41, 59, 60, 88, 89

F

failure, 53, 54, 68
faith, 45
Farm Security and Rural Investment Act, 18, 74
farmers, 51, 52
fast food, 16, 51
FDA, i, iii, vii, 1, 2, 3, 4, 5, 6, 7, 8, 9, 10, 11, 12, 13, 14, 15, 16, 17, 18, 19, 20, 21, 22, 23, 24, 25, 26, 27, 28, 29, 30, 31, 32, 33, 34, 35, 36, 37, 42, 46, 47, 48, 50, 51, 52,

53, 54, 55, 56, 57, 58, 59, 60, 61, 62, 63, 64, 67, 69, 70, 71, 72, 73, 87, 88, 89, 90, 91, 92
FDA approval, 3, 37, 59, 71
FDCA, 67, 69, 70, 71, 72, 73
fear, 5, 23, 34
February, 2, 5, 22, 42, 55, 58, 74, 75, 80, 81
federal courts, 68
federal funds, 52
federal government, 18, 24, 43, 51, 74, 85
federal law, 38, 40, 42, 68, 74, 77, 85
Federal Register, 15, 30
Federal Trade Commission, 4, 35, 66, 80, 82
Federal Trade Commission (FTC), 4, 66
Federal Trade Commission Act, 82
fee, 92
fees, 3, 19, 51, 53, 62, 63, 92
feet, 3, 7, 29, 30, 31, 82, 83, 84
fines, 49
First Amendment, 11, 28, 41, 42, 47, 71, 72, 83, 84
FL, 17
flavor, 32, 57, 80
flavors, 47
flexibility, 9
food, 8, 16, 44, 51, 67, 69, 92
Food and Drug Administration, vii, 1, 67, 68, 69, 87, 91
Food and Drug Administration (FDA), vii, 1
foreign nation, 81
fraud, 74, 78, 80
freedom, 84
Freedom of Information Act, 56
frustration, 40
FTC, 13, 35, 36, 60, 66
funding, 16, 19, 43, 51, 52, 75, 85
funds, 16, 17, 18, 50, 51, 53, 62, 73, 74, 92

G

games, 49
GAO, 18, 63, 74
general fund, 62
gifts, 8, 82
good faith, 45
government, 5, 17, 18, 19, 21, 23, 24, 28, 30, 32, 43, 45, 51, 52, 68, 74, 75, 81, 85, 93
Government Accountability Office, 17, 73
grants, 43, 85
groups, vii, 1, 2, 4, 5, 27, 28, 33, 46, 48, 68, 74, 79
Guatemala, 81
guidance, 45, 60
guidelines, 21

H

handling, 83, 84
harm, 9, 21, 36, 37, 58, 59, 66, 71, 81
harmful effects, 10
hazards, 39
health, 4, 8, 13, 14, 15, 16, 17, 19, 21, 24, 25, 26, 27, 32, 33, 34, 35, 36, 37, 38, 39, 41, 42, 47, 49, 50, 52, 53, 54, 57, 58, 59, 60, 63, 64, 65, 66, 68, 71, 73, 74, 76, 77, 82, 87, 89, 90, 91
Health and Human Services, vii, 1, 16, 29, 85, 89
Health and Human Services (HHS), 29, 85
health care, 8, 17, 52, 73, 74
health care system, 8
health effects, 63, 76, 89
health insurance, 16, 17, 74
hearing, 45, 58, 60, 87
heart, 10, 23, 66, 88
Heart, 23, 38
heart disease, 66, 88
heart valves, 10
HHS, 42, 43, 44, 46, 47, 85
hiring, 92
hospitals, 17, 74
House, 2, 6, 20, 26, 27, 30, 47, 53, 87
human, 15, 18, 49, 70

I

ice, 49
id, 5, 22, 23, 81
identification, 45

Illinois, 80
imagery, 6
images, 15, 49
immunity, 14, 51, 73, 80
implants, 10
implementation, 11, 17, 67
importer, 46, 54, 63
imports, 63
imprisonment, 44, 45
in vitro, 69
incentive, 90
incentive effect, 90
income, 19
income tax, 19
Indian, 63, 66
indication, 81
industrial, 83
industry, vii, 1, 4, 14, 15, 16, 17, 18, 19, 21, 25, 28, 29, 33, 34, 41, 47, 49, 51, 66, 68, 71, 74, 75, 76, 77, 78, 79, 82, 84
inflation, 16, 51, 92
infrastructure, 17, 74
initiation, 88
injuries, 81
injury, 10, 16, 18, 74, 80
inspection, 3, 49, 55
inspections, 16, 43, 50, 53, 85
instruction, 69
instruments, 9
insulin, 70
insurance, 16, 78
insurance companies, 78
Internet, 49, 56
interpretation, 12, 29, 71, 72
interstate, 44, 55, 63
interstate commerce, 44, 55
ions, 11, 46, 51

J

January, 7, 11, 78, 80, 81, 85
judge, 14
judges, 40
judgment, 10, 76, 80
jurisdiction, viii, 2, 3, 4, 8, 12, 13, 19, 60, 69, 70, 82
jury, 79
Justice Department, 11, 66

K

kidney, 88

L

LA, 82
labeling, 6, 9, 11, 29, 35, 37, 38, 41, 44, 46, 50, 54, 55, 59, 60, 61, 64, 65, 66, 69, 70, 71, 72, 78, 80
labor, 17, 18, 74
land, 31, 40
language, viii, 2, 4, 14, 18, 28, 40, 41, 42, 46
law, 12, 18, 19, 29, 32, 36, 37, 38, 39, 40, 41, 42, 43, 46, 51, 53, 58, 60, 64, 65, 66, 68, 69, 74, 76, 78, 82, 84, 85
laws, 16, 27, 38, 40, 41, 43, 46, 50, 51, 53, 61, 68, 72, 77, 82, 83, 84, 85
lawsuits, 14, 16, 17, 41, 51, 67, 68, 72, 73, 74, 77, 78, 79, 80
lead, 5, 8, 33, 36, 37, 78
legal issues, 2
legal protection, 17, 18
legislation, vii, 1, 2, 4, 5, 12, 13, 16, 19, 20, 21, 22, 23, 24, 25, 26, 27, 32, 33, 35, 36, 37, 40, 41, 46, 47, 72, 73, 89, 90, 92
legislative, 4, 5, 16, 19, 22, 25, 26, 40, 73
legislative proposals, 22
leukemia, 88
licensing, 7, 15, 17, 50, 52
life-threatening, 88
likelihood, 48, 59
limitation, 31, 43
limitations, 23, 80, 83
litigation, 76
lobbying, 22
local action, 52
local authorities, 49
local government, 17, 51, 52

location, 41, 46, 47
long-term, 24, 37, 48
loopholes, 91
lung, 38, 66, 78, 81, 88
lung cancer, 38, 78, 81
lung disease, 66, 88

M

machines, 7, 15, 29, 50
maintenance, 63
mandates, 37, 45, 49, 74
Manhattan, 31
manipulation, 76
manufacturer, 5, 8, 9, 18, 23, 35, 37, 39, 43, 45, 46, 53, 54, 55, 58, 59, 63, 70, 78, 85
manufacturing, 9, 21, 23, 49, 53, 56, 71, 78
market, 2, 3, 4, 5, 8, 10, 15, 19, 20, 22, 23, 33, 34, 35, 36, 37, 47, 49, 57, 58, 59, 63, 72, 76, 80, 90, 91
market share, 23, 63, 76
marketing, vii, 2, 4, 5, 6, 7, 8, 10, 13, 14, 17, 21, 23, 24, 25, 28, 29, 32, 35, 36, 46, 49, 56, 58, 69, 72, 73, 75, 77, 78, 82
markets, 58
marriage, 19
Massachusetts, 3, 29, 30, 41, 83, 84
measures, vii, 2, 3, 10, 25, 27, 52, 69, 71, 73, 75, 88
media, 49, 83
Medicaid, 14, 16, 17, 18, 72, 74
medical care, 18, 68, 74, 81
medical products, 91
Medicare, 75
medications, 69
membership, 61
memorandum of understanding, 66
merchandise, 49, 82
Mercury, 40
messages, 31, 47, 77
metropolitan area, 29, 30, 84
Minnesota, 73
minors, 6, 15, 16, 28, 41, 46, 49, 50, 56, 67, 68, 71, 82, 84, 85
misleading, 28, 37, 54, 74, 80
misleading statements, 74
Mississippi, 73
money, 74, 81
motion, 76, 77, 80
mouth, 66
MS, 17
mucosa, 71
music, 7, 49
myeloid, 88

N

naming, 82
narrowly tailored, 32, 85
nation, vii, 1, 5, 20, 23, 35
national, viii, 2, 4, 5, 14, 15, 16, 17, 18, 38, 41
National Institutes of Health (NIH), 35
Native Americans, 52
natural, 47, 57, 68, 76, 77
negligence, 77
New Jersey, 38
New York, 78
newspapers, 76
Nicaragua, 81
nicotine, vii, 2, 3, 5, 8, 9, 11, 14, 15, 19, 22, 24, 25, 28, 32, 33, 34, 35, 36, 48, 49, 51, 54, 57, 62, 64, 65, 66, 70, 73, 76, 80, 88, 89, 90
Nicotine, 33, 35, 36, 62, 66, 70
nicotine gum, 34, 89
nicotine patch, 34
nicotine replacement therapies, 34
nonsmokers, 66
normal, 34
normal conditions, 34
North Carolina, 11
nutrition, 69

O

online, 14, 20, 82
opposition, 20, 23
oral, 29, 34, 56, 84, 88
organizations, vii, 1, 20, 23, 44, 45, 76, 89, 93

oversight, 4
over-the-counter, 69

P

packaging, 6, 7, 15, 37, 46, 47, 50, 53, 63, 66, 68, 76, 82
pain, 79
pancreatic, 88
pancreatic cancer, 88
paper, 20, 21, 25
partnership, 23, 43
patients, 79, 87
penalties, 17, 18, 43, 44, 45, 46, 50, 73
penalty, 19, 44, 45
performance, 9, 15, 18, 27, 49
periodic, 54, 57
periodontitis, 88
permit, 10, 27, 29, 32, 33, 64, 71
personal, 16, 43
pesticide, 56, 57
pesticides, 57
petitioners, 84
pharmacological, 70
play, 31
pneumonia, 88
poisonous, 53, 91
policymakers, 24
population, 2, 19, 28, 31, 33, 34, 36, 37, 48, 55, 57, 58, 59, 81
population density, 31
power, 2, 67, 69
predictability, 21
pregnancy, 66
premature death, 88
prescription drug, 69
president, 22
pressure, 9
prevention, 17, 25, 28, 34, 53, 62, 69, 73, 89
prisoners, 43
prisons, 16, 51
private, 16, 17, 19, 51, 67, 68, 73, 78, 79, 93
product market, 2, 28
profits, 74, 75
program, 25, 46, 52, 91, 92
promote, 24, 50, 52, 64, 65, 90
property, 75
protection, 2, 11, 17, 19, 42, 58, 71, 84
public, vii, 1, 2, 3, 4, 5, 12, 13, 15, 16, 19, 21, 24, 25, 26, 28, 32, 33, 34, 36, 37, 38, 41, 42, 44, 45, 46, 47, 48, 49, 50, 51, 52, 54, 55, 57, 58, 59, 60, 61, 64, 65, 66, 71, 76, 82, 87, 88, 89, 90, 91, 92
public awareness, 50
public health, vii, 1, 2, 3, 4, 5, 12, 13, 19, 24, 25, 26, 28, 32, 33, 34, 37, 41, 42, 44, 45, 47, 48, 49, 50, 55, 57, 58, 61, 66, 71, 88, 89, 90, 91
Public Health Service, 42, 53, 85
public support, 90
Puerto Rico, 14, 72
punitive, 16, 79, 80

Q

quotas, 25, 52

R

racketeering, 74, 78
radio, 65, 68, 82
random, 16, 43, 53, 85
range, 9, 23, 34, 69
readership, 7, 8, 30, 49, 52
reagent, 69
reasoning, 22
recall, 18, 49, 58
recognition, 23, 28
record keeping, 91
recovery, 75
reduction, vii, 2, 16, 18, 27, 33, 36, 37, 50, 59
Reform Act, 63
regular, 24, 48, 78
regulation, vii, 2, 3, 4, 5, 10, 11, 15, 16, 18, 19, 20, 21, 22, 23, 24, 25, 28, 30, 32, 33, 40, 41, 42, 44, 45, 46, 49, 54, 55, 56, 57, 58, 60, 62, 84, 91, 92

regulations, 3, 6, 14, 28, 29, 30, 36, 37, 38, 40, 41, 42, 43, 44, 46, 50, 54, 55, 56, 60, 61, 63, 66, 71, 83, 84, 85, 92
regulatory framework, 5
regulatory requirements, 15
reimbursement, 17, 18, 51, 67, 72, 74
rejection, 26
relapse, 62
relatives, 73, 77
Republican, 47
research, 16, 22, 23, 24, 39, 51, 54, 75, 78, 89
residues, 56
resources, 90, 91, 92
respiratory, 34
restaurants, 16, 51
restitution, 74
retail, 7, 16, 24, 45, 46, 53, 56, 60, 66, 76, 82, 83, 84
revenue, 51, 62
Reynolds, 5, 17, 22, 23, 32, 76, 77, 78, 80
RICO, 68, 74, 75, 76, 77, 79
risk, 9, 10, 15, 16, 21, 23, 34, 35, 36, 37, 48, 49, 50, 53, 54, 57, 58, 59, 60, 61, 71, 78, 88, 90, 91
risks, 2, 15, 19, 21, 24, 28, 33, 34, 47, 48, 49, 50, 55, 57, 58, 60, 64, 65, 66, 77, 90

S

saccharin, 69
safety, 8, 9, 10, 18, 19, 69, 71, 90, 92
sales, 7, 11, 16, 27, 41, 42, 46, 50, 56, 66, 68, 77, 82, 83, 84, 85, 89
satellite, 82
satisfaction, 8
school, 3, 7, 29, 30, 31, 83
scientific community, 71
SCP, 22, 42
Secretary of Agriculture, 63
secrets, 56
security, 84
sedation, 8
Senate, 2, 4, 18, 19, 22, 26, 27, 42, 47, 52, 74
September 11, 76
series, 28
services, 7, 17, 74
settlements, 17
shareholders, 78
shares, 90
shipping, 63
signs, 78, 82
smoke, 3, 14, 20, 21, 22, 24, 32, 34, 35, 36, 47, 54, 61, 66, 76, 80, 89, 91
smokers, 5, 6, 16, 21, 22, 23, 33, 34, 35, 47, 51, 73, 75, 77, 78, 79, 80, 81, 88, 89
smoking, 6, 16, 17, 21, 29, 33, 34, 35, 36, 37, 38, 39, 41, 42, 47, 51, 64, 66, 75, 76, 77, 80, 81, 88, 89, 92
smoking cessation, 75, 89, 92
smuggling, 22, 63, 91
Social Security, 75
solutions, 89
spam, 82
speech, 11, 28, 30, 32, 71, 84
sponsor, 83
sports, 82
stages, 89
stakeholder groups, 2, 27
standards, vii, 2, 9, 15, 18, 21, 22, 24, 27, 32, 33, 40, 41, 43, 44, 46, 48, 49, 57, 61, 90, 91
state laws, 14, 17, 27, 41, 43, 68
state legislatures, 24
statute of limitations, 80
statutes, 12, 13, 16, 38, 42, 73, 82
statutory, viii, 2, 4, 9, 10, 11, 13, 14, 40, 70, 71
stock price, 78
stomach, 88
storage, 53
stress, 23
strokes, 66
substance abuse, 16, 42, 53, 85
substances, 59, 60
sudden infant death syndrome, 88
suffering, 79, 88
supplements, 69
suppression, 30
Supreme Court, vii, 2, 3, 4, 5, 11, 12, 13, 20, 21, 22, 28, 29, 30, 32, 38, 39, 40, 41, 67, 68, 70, 71, 77, 79, 80, 81, 83, 84

Surgeon General, 38, 47, 88, 89
surgical, 9
surveillance, 10, 18, 36, 37, 49, 60, 89
symptoms, 8

T

tar, 22, 24, 27, 35, 36, 64, 65, 66, 68, 76, 80
targets, 16, 17, 18, 50, 73, 82
tax increase, 19
tax rates, 63
teenagers, 6, 14
telephone, 82
television, 65, 68, 76, 82
television advertisements, 68
tenants, 52
Texas, 73, 87
theory, 70
third party, 18, 74
threat, 12
throat, 88
tobacco, vii, 1, 2, 3, 4, 5, 6, 7, 8, 9, 10, 11, 12, 13, 14, 15, 16, 17, 18, 19, 20, 21, 22, 23, 24, 25, 26, 27, 28, 29, 31, 32, 33, 34, 35, 36, 37, 41, 42, 43, 44, 45, 46, 47, 48, 49, 50, 51, 52, 53, 54, 55, 56, 57, 58, 59, 60, 61, 62, 63, 64, 65, 66, 67, 68, 70, 71, 72, 73, 74, 75, 76, 77, 78, 79, 80, 81, 82, 83, 84, 85, 88, 89, 90, 91, 92
tobacco smoke, 33, 50
tobacco toxins, 35
tort, 38, 80
toxic, vii, 2, 69
toxins, 35
trade, 3, 7, 49, 52, 56, 63, 68, 74, 76, 79, 80
training, 46
transactions, 50, 56, 63
transdermal patch, 70
transfer, 45
transportation, 82
treasury, 62
trial, 73, 75, 80, 83
tribal lands, 52
tribes, 63
trust fund, 51

U

Ukraine, 81
uniform, 41
uninsured, 16
unions, 17
United States, 24, 29, 40, 45, 46, 55, 63, 69, 75, 76, 77, 84, 87
urban areas, 31

V

vacancies, 92
varenicline, 89
ventilation, 35, 36
veterans, 52
Vice President, 22, 42
video games, 49
visible, 29, 83

W

war, 87
welfare, 87
wholesalers, 52
withdrawal, 8
workers, 62
worry, 23, 34
wrongdoing, 75

Y

yield, 33, 49, 54
young adults, 88

Z

zoning, 29